'An enjoyable and informative ...
illustrated with pithy examples of his own reasoning
encourages the reader to learn more about psychoanalysis's founding theorist and practitioner'.
– Susie Orbach, author of *Fat is a Feminist Issue* and many other books, most recently *In Therapy: The Unfolding Story*

'This book works through the fascinating string of ideas which Freud produced in trying to find access to the hidden unconscious area of the mind by which we all live. With this introductory text Janet Sayers provides comprehensive coverage of the many areas of human life and experience considered by Freud including his false starts, detours, and ways in which both he and his followers addressed issues in developmental and abnormal psychology as well as in the arts, social sciences, and in religion too'.
– Bob Hinshelwood, psychoanalyst and emeritus professor, University of Essex

SIGMUND FREUD

Sigmund Freud: The Basics is an easy-to-read introduction to the life and ideas of Sigmund Freud, the founder of psychoanalysis and a key figure in the history of psychology.

Janet Sayers provides an accessible overview of Freud's early life and work, beginning with his childhood. Her book includes the stories of his most famous patients: Dora, Little Hans, the Rat Man, Judge Schreber, and the Wolf Man. It also discusses Freud's key ideas such as psychosexual development, the Oedipus complex, and psychoanalytic treatment. Sayers then covers Freud's later work, with a description of his observations about depression, trauma and the death instinct, as well as his 1923 theory of the id, ego, and superego. The book includes a glossary of key terms and concludes with examples of how psychoanalysis has been applied to the study of art, literature, film, anthropology, religion, sociology, gender politics, and racism.

Sigmund Freud: The Basics offers an essential introduction for students from all backgrounds seeking to understand Freud's ideas and for general readers with an interest in psychology. For those already familiar with Freudian ideas, it offers a helpful guide to their interdisciplinary applications and context not least today.

Janet Sayers is emeritus professor of psychoanalytic psychology at the University of Kent in Canterbury where she also works as a clinical psychologist for the National Health Service. Her previous Routledge books include *Art, Psychoanalysis and Adrian Stokes: A Biography*; *Freud's Art: Psychoanalysis Retold*; and *Boy Crazy: Remembering Adolescence, Therapies and Dreams*.

THE BASICS

The Basics is a highly successful series of accessible guidebooks which provide an overview of the fundamental principles of a subject area in a jargon-free and undaunting format.

Intended for students approaching a subject for the first time, the books both introduce the essentials of a subject and provide an ideal springboard for further study. With over 50 titles spanning subjects from artificial intelligence (AI) to women's studies, *The Basics* are an ideal starting point for students seeking to understand a subject area.

Each text comes with recommendations for further study and gradually introduces the complexities and nuances within a subject.

MODERNISM
LAURA WINKIEL

NUMERICAL COGNITION
ANDRÉ KNOPS

NARRATIVE
BRONWEN THOMAS

POETRY (THIRD EDITION)
JEFFREY WAINWRIGHT

POVERTY
BENT GREVE

THE QUR'AN (SECOND EDITION)
MASSIMO CAMPANINI

RESEARCH METHODS (SECOND EDITION)
NICHOLAS WALLIMAN

SEMIOTICS
DANIEL CHANDLER

SPECIAL EDUCATIONAL NEEDS AND DISABILITY (THIRD EDITION)
JANICE WEARMOUTH

SPORT MANAGEMENT
ROBERT WILSON AND MARK PIEKARZ

SPORTS COACHING
LAURA PURDY

TRANSLATION
JULIANE HOUSE

TOWN PLANNING
TONY HALL

WOMEN'S STUDIES (SECOND EDITION)
BONNIE G. SMITH

SIGMUND FREUD
JANET SAYERS

For a full list of titles in this series, please visit www.routledge.com/The-Basics/book-series/B

SIGMUND FREUD

THE BASICS

Janet Sayers

Routledge
Taylor & Francis Group
LONDON AND NEW YORK

First published 2021
by Routledge
2 Park Square, Milton Park, Abingdon, Oxon OX14 4RN

and by Routledge
52 Vanderbilt Avenue, New York, NY 10017

Routledge is an imprint of the Taylor & Francis Group, an informa business

© 2021 Janet Sayers

The right of Janet Sayers to be identified as author of this work has been asserted by her in accordance with sections 77 and 78 of the Copyright, Designs and Patents Act 1988.

All rights reserved. No part of this book may be reprinted or reproduced or utilised in any form or by any electronic, mechanical, or other means, now known or hereafter invented, including photocopying and recording, or in any information storage or retrieval system, without permission in writing from the publishers.

Trademark notice: Product or corporate names may be trademarks or registered trademarks, and are used only for identification and explanation without intent to infringe.

British Library Cataloguing-in-Publication Data
A catalogue record for this book is available from the British Library

Library of Congress Cataloging-in-Publication Data
Names: Sayers, Janet, author.
Title: Sigmund Freud: the basics / Janet Sayers.
Description: New York : Routledge, 2020. | Series: The basics |
Includes bibliographical references and index.
Identifiers: LCCN 2020016067 (print) | LCCN 2020016068 (ebook) |
ISBN 9780367340117 (hardback) | ISBN 9780367340124 (paperback) |
ISBN 9780429323447 (ebook)
Subjects: LCSH: Freud, Sigmund, 1856–1939. | Psychotherapy–History.
Classification: LCC BF173.F85 S279 2020 (print) |
LCC BF173.F85 (ebook) | DDC 150.19/52–dc23
LC record available at https://lccn.loc.gov/2020016067
LC ebook record available at https://lccn.loc.gov/2020016068

ISBN: 978-0-367-34011-7 (hbk)
ISBN: 978-0-367-34012-4 (pbk)
ISBN: 978-0-429-32344-7 (ebk)

Typeset in Bembo
by Newgen Publishing UK

For Esme, Neve, and Nina

CONTENTS

List of figures	xii
Acknowledgements	xiii
Preface	xv

PART I PRE-PSYCHOANALYTIC FREUD — 1

1	Childhood and youth	3
2	Talking cure	8
3	Resistance and repression	12
4	Repressed abuse	17
5	Wishful fantasy	20
	Conclusions to Part I	26

PART II UNCONSCIOUS-CONSCIOUS DYNAMICS — 27

6	Dreams	29
7	Freudian slips	37
8	Jokes	43

9	Sex	47
	Conclusions to Part II	54

PART III PSYCHOANALYTIC CASE STUDIES   55

10	Dora's dreams	57
11	Hans's phobia	63
12	The Rat Man's obsession	70
13	Schreber's schizophrenia	76
14	The Wolf Man's nightmare	85
	Conclusions to Part III	90

PART IV CONSOLIDATING PSYCHOANALYSIS   93

15	Freud versus Jung	95
16	Sex and repression	99
17	Freudian symbols	102
18	More about sex	106
19	Symptom formation	111
20	Psychoanalytic treatment	114
	Conclusions to Part IV	124

PART V WAR AND ITS PSYCHOANALYTIC AFTERMATH   125

21	Mourning and melancholia	127
22	Trauma and the death instinct	133
23	Oedipus, castration, penis envy	138
24	Id-ego-superego	142
	Conclusions to Part V	150

PART VI BEYOND CLINICAL PSYCHOANALYSIS   151

25	Art, literature, film	153
26	Anthropology	162

27	Religion	169
28	Sociology	174
29	Gender politics	180
30	Racism	186
	Conclusions to Part VI	190

Glossary	192
References	206
Index	215

FIGURES

6.1	Brain lobes diagram	33
7.1	Freudian slip © Mike Monahan/Shutterstock.com	38
9.1	PEANUTS © Peanuts Worldwide LLC. Dist.	49
24.1	Two of Richard's empire drawings, courtesy Melanie Klein Trust	147

ACKNOWLEDGEMENTS

I first learnt about Freud as a teenager at Dartington Hall School where his grandsons, Lucian and Clement, were pupils in the 1930s. Thanks to a maths teacher, Michael Bailey, recommending Freud's *Introductory Lectures on Psycho-Analysis* as antidote to teenage boredom, I learnt about Freudian slips, jokes, symbols, dreams, symptoms, and about Freud's approach to psychoanalytic treatment. I also learnt about psychoanalysis at Dartington from a former pupil, the psychoanalyst Susan Isaacs-Elmhirst, giving a talk about her work at the Paddington Green Hospital for Children.

I acquired more knowledge about Freud and psychoanalysis from teachers at Cambridge University, notably John Wisdom, Marie Singer, and John Forrester; from staff at London's Tavistock Clinic including John Bowlby, R. D. Laing, David Riley, and Caroline Garland; and from the psychoanalysts Brenda Morrison, Dana Birksted-Breen, Ronald Britton, Martha Papadakis, and many others before, during, and since my psychoanalytic training at the British Association of Psychotherapists.

To all this has been added learning about the continuing relevance of Freud today from patients and colleagues with whom I work as a clinical psychologist for the National Health Service, and from students I teach at the University of Kent in Canterbury. In addition

I continue to learn a great deal relevant to Freud from relatives and friends, and from discussions of draft chapters of this book with Sarah Carter, Mary Evans, Judith Hattaway, Lyn Innes, Jan Pahl, and Clare Ungerson.

Whether or not they agree or would have agreed with what I have written in the following pages, responsibility for which rests entirely with me, my thanks to all of the above and to my editor, Susannah Frearson at Routledge. Their help has been invaluable.

PREFACE

Sigmund Freud's ideas are all around us. Although he died over eighty years ago, notions such as Freudian slips and symbols still pepper everyday talk. So too do his revolutionary ideas about the repressed unconscious, infant sexuality, abnormal psychology, and the Oedipus complex. It still often seems that this complex – the childhood wish to get rid of one's father so as to have one's mother to oneself – dominates the subsequent love life of both sexes, women as well as men. And, of course, there is also Freud's radical innovation into psychiatry and psychotherapy with his free association based talking cure method of treating neurotic and other psychological ills.

How did this and other aspects of the revolution which Freud brought about and which is still ubiquitous in our twenty-first century world develop? In answering this question I recount this revolution's basics in terms, more or less, of its genesis over the course of Freud's life. In doing so I quote a great deal from his own writings and provide reference details so readers can pursue particular aspects of his work in more detail.

I begin with Freud's early life and work before going on to describe his account of unconscious-conscious dynamics in everyday life. I follow this with his five major case studies; his consolidation of psychoanalytic theory and practice; changes he made to psychoanalysis during and following the 1914–1918 World War; and their legacy for psychotherapy today. Last but not least, I end with ways in which Freud and his followers have applied his clinically derived ideas in thinking and writing about art, literature, and film, and about anthropology, religion, sociology, gender politics, and racism.

PART I
PRE-PSYCHOANALYTIC FREUD

This part focuses on the early years of Freud's life before he founded psychoanalysis in 1900. It begins with his birth in Moravia on 6 May 1856; the family's move, when he was nearly four, to Vienna; the start of his university studies in 1873; his research in physiology, anatomy, and into medical uses of cocaine before going in October 1885 to study hysteria with Martin Charcot in Paris; his return to Vienna, where in April 1886 he begins work as a doctor specializing in nervous disorders; and where that September he marries Martha Bernays, with whom he has six children. His first book, *On Aphasia*, is published in 1891, followed by the publication in 1895 of his and Breuer's book *Studies on Hysteria*. In it Freud announces his discovery of the repressed unconscious erotic cause of hysteria. He follows this with his 'seduction theory' that hysteria is due to repressed memory of being sexually abused as a very young child – a theory which he almost immediately rejects in favour of arguing that, whether or not they are sexually abused, all young children experience Oedipal jealousy of their father for love of their mother, a theory to which he adds evidence regarding the wishful fantasy basis of memories of early childhood.

CHILDHOOD AND YOUTH

Sigmund Freud's parents, Jacob and Amalia, were Jewish. They came from Galicia, a Polish part of the Austro-Hungarian empire, and were living in a single rented room above a blacksmith's business in Freiburg, Moravia (now in the Czech Republic), when Sigmund was born on 6 May 1856.

Jacob was then forty-one, worked in the family wool merchant business, and already had two sons, Emmanuel and Philipp, by his first marriage. Amalia, by contrast, was only twenty-one when, as Jacob's third wife, she gave birth to Sigmund. He was the favourite of her eight children. They included his brother, Julius, who died aged seven months, and Sigmund's sister, Anna, born in December 1858.

Sigmund's other siblings came later after 'a catastrophe' in the family business in which Jacob 'lost his fortune' when, due perhaps to growing anti-Semitism in Catholic Freiburg during the 1859 Austro–Italian war, the family moved in August 1859 to Leipzig (Freud, 1899, p. 312). From Leipzig they moved again. In March 1860 they went to Vienna. Here they settled in a poor Jewish quarter, Leopoldstadt. And it was in Vienna that Amalia gave birth to Sigmund's other siblings, namely his sisters Rosa, Mitzi, Dolfi, and Pauli, and his youngest sibling, Alexander, born in April 1866.

By then Sigmund had suffered the indignity, aged seven or eight years old, of peeing in his parents' bedroom to which his father had responded by predicting, 'The boy will come to nothing' (Freud, 1900, p. 216). Freud also recalled being appalled, a couple of years later, by the following incident of which he said,

> [My father] told me a story to show me how much better things were now than they had been in his days. 'When I was a young man', he said, 'I went for a walk one Saturday in the streets of your birthplace [Freiburg]; I was well dressed, and had a new fur cap on my head. A Christian came up to me and with a single blow knocked off my cap into the mud and shouted: "Jew! Get off the pavement!"' 'And what did you do?' I asked. 'I went into the roadway and picked up my cap', was his quiet reply. This struck me as unheroic conduct on the part of the big, strong man who was holding the little boy by the hand. I contrasted this situation with another which fitted my feelings better: the scene in which Hannibal's father, Hamilcar Barca, made his boy swear before the household altar to take vengeance on the Romans. Ever since that time Hannibal has had a place in my phantasies. (Freud, 1900, p. 197)

Freud (as I will now call him) had good reason to hope that, despite being Jewish, he might do well in life just as Hannibal had many centuries before. Prior to Freud's birth, the revolutions of 1848 in Europe had been followed by the Austro–Hungarian empire, of which Vienna was the capital, granting full civil and political rights to Jews. Freud could therefore realistically hope to make a career for himself in Vienna as a doctor or lawyer.

The Jewish population in Vienna was also increasing. During Freud's years at secondary school, where he was top of his class for seven years in succession, the proportion of Jewish to other students increased from '44 to 73 percent of the total school population' (Gay, 1988, p. 20). There was also considerable anti-Semitism, not least when in May 1873 a financial crisis occurred resulting in bankruptcies and business failures for which the Viennese Jews were 'accused of destabilizing the markets' (Roudinesco, 2016, p. 25).

The same year Freud registered, aged seventeen, as a student at Vienna University where he later recalled,

> I found that I was expected to feel myself inferior and an alien because I was a Jew. I refused absolutely to do the first of these things. I have never been able to see why I should feel ashamed of my descent or, as people were beginning to say, of my 'race'. I put up, without much regret, with my non-acceptance into the community; for it seemed to me that in spite of this exclusion an active fellow-worker could not fail to find some nook or cranny in the framework of humanity. These first impressions at the University, however, had one consequence which was afterwards to prove important; for at an early age I was made familiar with the fate of being in the Opposition and of being put under the ban of the 'compact majority'. The foundations were thus laid for a certain degree of independence of judgement. (Freud, 1925c, p. 9)

Being his mother's favourite child must have helped. He had a room to himself while his parents, together with their six other children, had to make do with three bedrooms between them in the larger apartment to which Jacob moved the family during Freud's student days. Furthermore, so devoted seemingly were Freud's parents to him that, when he complained of the noise made by his sister Anna's piano playing, the piano was removed.

Freud was not keen on music. But he certainly benefited from other aspects of the artistic and cultural life of late nineteenth-century Vienna where there were many Jewish publishers, editors, gallery owners, theatre and music promoters, poets, novelists, conductors, virtuosos, painters, scientists, philosophers, and historians. In later life Freud's friends included the novelists Arthur Schnitzler and Stefan Zweig, and he was consulted in his work as a psychoanalyst by the composer Gustav Mahler.

As a student, Freud's travels took him in early 1875 to England where he visited his half-brothers, Emanuel and Philipp, in Manchester. Following his return to Vienna, and thanks to work there in the zoology laboratory of Carl Claus, Freud did research, beginning in March 1876, in an experimental laboratory of marine biology in Trieste into the sexual organs of eels.

On his return to Vienna he did research in a laboratory headed by the German doctor and physiologist Ernst Brücke. Here, as well as getting to know a fellow researcher, Josef Breuer, who would become a major influence on his subsequent clinical work, Freud's research included evolutionary-based investigation of the nervous system of fish, this resulting in one of his first scientific publications.

Following a year's compulsory military service in 1879 and 1880, and after completing his medical degree in 1881, Freud continued doing physiology research with Brücke. But this ended when, after falling in love with, and getting engaged in June 1882 to marry one of his sister's friends, Martha Bernays, Freud was persuaded by Brücke to get the medical training needed to qualify as a doctor so as to earn the money needed to support a family.

To this end Freud got work in Vienna's general hospital. Here, while completing his medical training and qualification, he did research with the psychiatrist, neuropathologist, and anatomist Theodor Meynert. In May 1884, Freud achieved the rank of junior doctor and soon after qualified as a university lecturer.

By then he had done research into medical uses of cocaine. This resulted in an article, 'On Coca', published in June 1884. But his hopes of doing well in research into cocaine were, it seems, crushed by another researcher, Carl Koller, being credited with discovering the value of cocaine as an anaesthetic in eye surgery. Freud's research into cocaine was also brought to an end, apparently, due to what in retrospect turned out to be his ill-judged prescription of cocaine to ease problems of his friend Ernst von Fleischl-Marxow.

Freud had meanwhile learnt about his above-mentioned friend Josef Breuer's treatment of a case of hysteria. This may have contributed to Freud going, in October 1885, to study in Paris with Martin Charcot. By then Charcot was famous not only for demonstrating that hysteria occurs in men as well as in women. He was also famous for overturning previous neurological accounts of this condition by using hypnosis to demonstrate its psychological cause.

After leaving Paris in February 1886, Freud studied children's diseases in Berlin before returning to Vienna. Here, that April, he began work as a doctor specializing in the treatment of patients with hysteria and other nervous or psychological problems. Money from this work, together with financial help from his fiancée Martha Bernays's family, enabled him to marry her that September.

Their first child, Mathilde, was born the following October. They went on to have five more children – Jean-Martin, Oliver, Ernst, Sophie, and Anna. By the time Anna was born, on 3 December 1895, Freud's first book – an account of the psychology of aphasia affecting the ability to speak, read, and write – had been published. The same year, 1891, the Freud family moved to a large flat in Vienna, Bergasse 19. It remained Freud's home for the next forty-seven years.

> SUMMARY: Born in Freiburg on 6 May 1856, Freud was brought up with his six younger siblings in Vienna. Here, after becoming a university student in 1873, he did research in physiology and anatomy, qualified as a doctor, and studied hysteria in Paris with the then leading specialist in this condition, Martin Charcot. In April 1886 Freud began work as a doctor specializing in the treatment of nervous disorders including hysteria. That September he married his fiancée, Martha Bernays, with whom he went on to have six children.

TALKING CURE

Freud is often credited with inventing the talking cure treatment of psychological ills. In fact, however, the term 'talking cure' was first used by his friend Josef Breuer's patient Anna O during her treatment by Breuer, which began in December 1880, and about which Breuer first told Freud in November 1882.

In a jointly written article the two men recounted their finding that the psychological trauma causing the symptoms of hysteria could be discovered by persuading the patient to recall, under hypnosis, the first occurrence of their symptoms. Examples included an involuntary 'clacking' noise made with her tongue emitted by one of Freud's patients, Emmy von N. Under hypnosis it transpired that this symptom began when, despite wanting to keep particularly quiet so as not to waken her sick daughter, Emmy found herself making this noise against her will.

Breuer and Freud described other symptoms of hysteria as 'symbolic' of the psychological trauma causing them. Examples included vomiting as symbol of 'moral disgust'. They found that, provided the patient recalled under hypnosis *both* emotionally *and* in words the psychological trauma causing their symptoms of hysteria, these symptoms 'immediately and permanently disappeared' (Breuer & Freud, 1893, pp. 5, 6).

Why, though, were patients not conscious, without hypnosis, of the psychological trauma causing each of their symptoms of hysteria? The answer, according to Breuer and Freud, was that the emotional experience evoked by the trauma involved was not sufficiently expressed or 'abreacted' at the time it occurred. There was therefore no cathartic release, as they called it, of this trauma's emotional effect. Sometimes, they argued, this lack of release was due to the trauma occurring when the patient was in a day-dreaming 'hypnoid' state of mind such that it remained unconscious and cut off from conscious awareness (Breuer & Freud, 1893, pp. 8, 12).

Another explanation was that the nature of the trauma prevented the emotion it evoked being expressed at the time it occurred. An example was a man for whom the traumatic cause of his hysterical symptoms first occurred when he was unable to express the full strength of the fury evoked in him by the trauma of his work supervisor's behaviour towards him. Insufficiently abreacted at the time, and cut off from consciousness, this trauma was instead expressed by this man in the form of outbursts of hysteria in which 'he collapsed and fell into a frenzy of rage' (Breuer & Freud, 1893, p. 14).

Through enabling patients to recall, under hypnosis, both verbally and emotionally the full force of the trauma causing their symptoms, this force was purged. Furthermore, claimed Breuer and Freud, this had the effect of restoring to 'normal consciousness' the previously unconscious trauma causing the patient's ills (Breuer & Freud, 1893, p. 17).

Breuer illustrated this method of treatment in detail with the example of Anna O, whose manifest bodily symptoms of hysteria included

> [P]araphasia, a convergent squint, severe disturbances of vision, paralyses (in the form of contractures), complete in the right upper and both lower extremities, partial in the left upper extremity, paresis of the neck muscles. (Breuer, 1895a, p. 22)

For each of these symptoms Breuer persuaded Anna to recall, under hypnosis, in feelings and words its traumatic cause.

In connection with one of these symptoms – namely paralysis of her right arm – Breuer recalled, on the basis of what Anna told him, the following occasion of its first appearance.

> In July, 1880, while he was in the country, her father fell seriously ill of a sub-pleural abscess. Anna shared the duties of nursing him with her mother. She once woke up during the night in great anxiety about the patient [her father], who was in a high fever; and she was under the strain of expecting the arrival of a surgeon from Vienna who was to operate. Her mother had gone away for a short time and Anna was sitting at the bedside with her right arm over the back of her chair. She fell into a waking dream and saw a black snake coming towards the sick man from the wall to bite him. [...] She tried to keep the snake off, but it was as though she was paralysed. Her right arm, over the back of the chair, had gone to sleep [...] When the snake vanished, in her terror she tried to pray. But language failed her [...] Next day, in the course of a game, she threw a quoit into some bushes; and when she went to pick it out, a bent branch revived her hallucination of the snake, and simultaneously her right arm became rigidly extended. Thenceforward the same thing invariably occurred whenever the hallucination was recalled by some object with a more or less snake-like appearance. (Breuer, 1895a, pp. 38–39)

By enabling Anna to fully experience both emotionally and verbally the snake trauma causing her paralysed right arm symptom of hysteria, Breuer brought about the disappearance of this symptom.

He adopted a similar talking cure treatment method in treating Anna's other symptoms of hysteria. Years after her cure she became well known as a leading women's rights campaigner, Berthe Pappenheim. Further details about her life and treatment by Breuer can be found in, for instance, Lisa Appignanesi and John Forrester's book, *Freud's Women*.

> SUMMARY: Together with Breuer, Freud argued in 1893 that talking cure treatment of hysteria entailed getting patients to recall under hypnosis both verbally and emotionally the full

force of the trauma causing their symptoms of hysteria – a trauma that was otherwise unconscious because it occurred when the patient was in a day-dreaming or hypnoid state of mind. Breuer illustrated this perspective on hysteria with the case of Anna O.

3

RESISTANCE AND REPRESSION

By the time Breuer's detailed account of Anna O's talking cure treatment was published, Freud had begun to forge a different theory of hysteria. Breuer attributed its symptoms to their traumatic cause occurring when the patient was in a daydreaming or hypnoid state of mind. It was for this reason, he argued, that Anna was unconscious of the traumatic cause of her symptoms of hysteria.

Freud, by contrast, argued that patients were unconscious of the cause of their symptoms of hysteria because they had repressed this cause through 'an act of will' (Freud, 1894, p. 46). Indicative, in Freud's view, of patients repressing the cause of their ills was their resistance to being hypnotized. Faced with this resistance, he was heartened by learning from a French doctor, Hippolyte Bernheim, that people can recall in full consciousness what occurs to them when they have been hypnotized provided they are sufficiently pressed to do so.

Devising a seemingly somewhat modified version of Bernheim's pressure technique, Freud said of its use in his talking cure treatment of patients who resisted hypnosis,

> When I reached a point at which, after asking a patient some question such as 'How long have you had this symptom?' or: 'what was its origin?', I was met with the answer: 'I really don't know', I proceeded as follows. I placed my hand on the patient's forehead or took her head between my hands and said: 'You will think of it under the pressure of my hand. At the moment at which I relax my pressure you will see something in front of you or something will come into your head. Catch hold of it. It will be what we are looking for. – Well, what have you seen or what has occurred to you?' (Freud, 1895b, p. 110)

Using this technique – the forerunner of his psychoanalytic treatment method of free association (of which more below) – Freud learnt what he described as the repressed unconscious cause of the hysterical symptoms of an English governess patient, Lucy R. It involved her having repressed and driven out of her mind her having 'fallen in love with her employer' because it was, she said, 'incompatible with her pride' (Freud, 1894, p. 48).

Conflict about love or sex, as Freud put it, was the cause of another of his patient's hysterical ills. Aged twenty-four, and referred to by Freud as Elisabeth von R, this patient's bodily symptoms of hysteria, for which he checked there was no organic cause, consisted of pain in her legs and difficulty in walking. Faced with her resistance to being hypnotized, Freud used his pressure technique. He told her when he applied pressure to her head, presumably with his hand, that she must tell him 'faithfully whatever appeared before her inner eye or passed through her memory at the moment of the pressure' (Freud, 1895b, p. 145).

At first she resisted and remained silent for a long time. Then, in response to Freud's insistence, she recalled in connection with the pain in her legs an evening when, instead of staying home to look after her very ill father, she enjoyed a romantic evening with a young suitor. She was accordingly appalled, on returning home later that evening, to discover that during her absence her father had become much more seriously ill. Of the resulting turbulence in her mind, Freud said,

> The contrast between the blissful feelings she had allowed herself to enjoy on that occasion and the worsening of her father's state which had met her on her return home constituted a conflict, a situation of incompatibility. The outcome of this conflict was that the erotic idea [involving her suitor] was repressed from association and the affect attaching to that idea was used to intensify or revive a physical pain which was present simultaneously or shortly before. (Freud, 1895b, pp. 146–147)

Why, though, Elisabeth's difficulty in walking? In connection with this symptom she recalled an occasion when, after a long walk with her sister's husband, this difficulty became particularly intense. It was also very severe when, a few days after this walk, dwelling on her loneliness and family problems, she fervently wished she could be as happy as her sister.

Freud also noticed that one day, when he was treating Elisabeth, the pain in her legs returned when she happened to hear the voice of her sister's husband in the next room. In answer to Freud then asking her when the pain in her legs first started, she recalled further memories about this man.

They culminated in her describing an occasion when staying with her family in Gastein they learnt that her sister was seriously ill near Vienna. They accordingly returned as fast as they could to see this sister. Of Elisabeth's recollection of this event, Freud said,

> I asked her whether during the journey [from Gastein to Vienna] she had thought of the grievous possibility which was afterwards realized. She answered that she had carefully avoided the thought, but she believed that her mother had from the beginning expected the worst. – Her memories now went to their arrival in Vienna, the impression made on them by the relatives who met them, the short journey from Vienna to the summer resort in its neighbourhood where her sister lived, their reaching there in the evening, the hurried walk through the garden to the door of the small garden house, the silence within and the oppressive darkness, how her brother-in-law was not there to receive them, and how they stood before the bed and looked at her sister as she lay there dead. At that moment

> of dreadful certainty that her beloved sister was dead without bidding them farewell and without her having eased her last days with her care – at that very moment another thought had shot through Elisabeth's mind, and now forced itself irresistibly upon her once more, like a flash of lightning in the dark: 'Now he is free again and I can be his wife'. (Freud, 1895b, p. 156)

Elisabeth nevertheless resisted recovery of 'this repressed idea' to consciousness. Why? Because, claimed Freud, it conflicted too much with love of her sister and grief at her death. Elisabeth also resisted acknowledging the truth of Freud's claim that, as he put it, 'So for a long time you had been in love with your brother-in-law' (Freud, 1895b, p. 157).

Nevertheless, with help from Freud, she was able to admit her love for this man. She was also able to experience the full force of the emotion involved. Previously, according to Freud, this emotion had been repressed and was unconscious in her. It was, said Freud, the conversion of this repressed and unconscious emotion into bodily form that caused Elisabeth's hysterical symptoms – her pain in her legs and difficulty in walking.

Reflecting on the tale that emerged from enabling Elisabeth and other patients to overcome their resistance to becoming conscious of the repressed unconscious cause of their bodily symptoms of hysteria, Freud observed,

> [I]t still strikes me myself as strange that the case studies I write should read like short stories and that, as one might say, they lack the serious stamp of science. I must console myself with the reflection that the nature of the subject is evidently responsible for this, rather than any preference of my own. (Freud, 1895b, p. 160).

That said, Freud went on to point out that patients sometimes objected to his treatment method that, whether or not their psychological ills were due to a repressed and unconscious cause, these ills were due to external circumstances which they could not change. In answering this objection Freud told his patients,

> No doubt fate would find it easier than I do to relieve you of your illness. But you will be able to convince yourself that much will be gained if we succeed in transforming your hysterical misery into common unhappiness. With a mental life that has been restored to health you will be better armed against that unhappiness. (Freud, 1895c, p. 305).

More importantly perhaps for psychoanalysis was the fact that, through experiencing his patients' resistance to recalling the origin of their ills, Freud discovered an aspect of the unconscious mind about which nothing, or precious little, had ever been noted in all the many previous observations made about this aspect of human psychology. 'I gave the name *repression* to this hypothetical process', Freud later said of this inaccessible aspect of the unconscious mind, 'and I considered that it was proved by the undeniable existence of resistance' (Freud, 1910a, p. 24, italics in original).

SUMMARY: The resistance of his patients to being hypnotized led Freud to use a pressure technique to discover the cause of their bodily symptoms of hysteria. This resulted in his arriving at the theory that it is repression of erotic or sexual desire and its conversion into bodily form that is the cause of these symptoms.

REPRESSED ABUSE

Breuer's account of Anna O, and Freud's account of Lucy R and Elisabeth von R can be found in their 1895 book, *Studies on Hysteria*. Also in this book is Freud's account of an eighteen-year-old patient, Katharina, whose symptoms of hysteria originated, it transpired, in her having been sexually abused by her father when she was fourteen.

Other examples of sexual abuse causing psychological ills included for Freud a patient, Emma Eckstein. In her case these ills included a phobia of going into shops alone. This phobia began, she said, when as a teenager she went into a shop alone and saw two shop assistants laughing.

Why, though, did this seemingly innocent episode cause her phobia? Because, it transpired, the shop assistant's laughter reminded her, and gave new sexual meaning by 'deferred action' now she was sexually mature, to an incident when, aged eight, she went into a shop alone and the shopkeeper grinned as he grabbed at her through her clothes (Freud, 1895a, p. 356). In addition, she now guiltily recalled, despite his having thus sexually assaulted her, she again went into his sweet shop alone.

Freud recounted this case example in a paper, 'Project for a scientific psychology', a draft of which he sent to his close doctor friend,

Wilhelm Fliess, in 1895. That April he also gave a lecture in which he recounted the cases of eighteen patients – twelve women and six men – who recalled that their symptoms of hysteria or neurosis had begun following what he regarded as more or less trivial experiences occurring after they reached puberty. Of the more trivial examples of these experiences he said,

> In one of my women patients it turned out that her neurosis was based on the experience of a boy of her acquaintance stroking her hand tenderly and, at another time, pressing his knee against her dress as they sat side by side at table, while his expression let her see that he was doing something forbidden. For another young lady, simply hearing a riddle which suggested an obscene answer had been enough to provoke the first anxiety attack and with it to start the illness. (Freud, 1896b, pp. 200–201)

However upsetting such experience might seem to us, they were, in Freud's view, neither sufficiently 'relevant' nor sufficiently 'traumatic' to have caused his patients' symptoms of hysteria. To arrive at a more relevant and traumatic cause of these symptoms, he pressed his patients to recall earlier 'associations' from their childhood which might account for them (Freud, 1896, pp. 193, 195).

On this basis he arrived at 'the thesis' that in every case of hysteria the patient's symptoms were due to their having undergone 'one or more occurrences of premature sexual experience' when they were aged eight, three, two, or even only one year old (Freud, 1896, pp. 203, 212). This premature sexual experience involved the patient having been sexually abused, or seduced as Freud put it, as an infant or young child by a stranger, by someone who then looked after them, or by an older child who had themselves been sexually seduced or abused. Had this not happened, Freud insisted, the patient would have remained sexually innocent until the onset of puberty.

Why though did the symptoms of hysteria in these patients take the bodily form of 'choking and vomiting', 'disgust at food', 'painful […] sensation accompanying defaecation', or 'diverse sensations of the genital organs' (Freud, 1896, p. 214)? Because, said Freud, with these bodily symptoms the patients reproduced the oral, anal, or genital sexual abuse of which they had been victims as very young children.

But sexual abuse of young children is very frequent, Freud rather surprisingly observed. Why then is hysteria due to this abuse not more frequent? Because, he claimed, in what has come to be known as his seduction theory of hysteria, this condition only occurs when memory of its sexually abusive cause in infancy or early childhood is repressed such that it becomes unconscious and is converted into the bodily symptoms of hysteria.

> *SUMMARY:* In 1896 Freud developed his seduction or repressed abuse theory of hysteria. Pressing patients to recall the cause of their hysterical symptoms, he discovered their associations led in every case to memories of being sexually abused as infants or young children. Repression of these memories such that they became unconscious resulted, he argued, in their being converted from psychological into bodily hysterical form.

Handwritten notes:

→ Is this the start of CBT - it is the meaning in which we give events that accounts for psych illness.

Also - mysogyny? Freud decided what was severe and what was trivial experiences of womens SA, being a man himself.

5

WISHFUL FANTASY

> *[handwritten annotation:] made the distinction
> 1) Different ages of maturation/development
> 2) Different types of neurosis*

When Freud announced his seduction or repressed abuse theory of hysteria in April 1896, it was denounced by an expert in sexual perversions, Richard Krafft-Ebing, as a scientific fairy tale. Undeterred, Freud added to this theory that May the claim that, while hysteria was due to sexual abuse of the patient when they were eighteen months to four years old, obsessional neurosis was due to sexual abuse of the patient when they were four to eight years old, and paranoia was due to sexual abuse of the patient when they were eight to fourteen years old.

The following April 1897, however, he speculated that his patients' repressed memories of having been sexually abused might have been the product of wishful fantasy resulting from things they had heard 'at an early age' (Freud, 1892–1899, p. 244). He nevertheless credited that month a woman patient telling him

> [H]er supposedly otherwise high-minded and respectable father regularly took her to bed when she was from 8 to 12 years old and misused her without penetrating ('made her wet', nocturnal visits). She felt anxiety even at the time. A sister, six years her senior, had told her years afterwards that she had had the same experiences with

> their father. A cousin told her that when she was fifteen she had had to fend off her grandfather's embraces. (Freud, 1892–1899, p. 247)

She was quite prepared to believe Freud's suggestion that she probably suffered worse abuse in her earliest childhood.

Yet the following month, May 1897, Freud argued that his patients' memories of being sexually abused in their early childhood were due to 'embellishments' of what they had heard as children. They were aimed at 'self-exoneration'. They were means by which patients sought to defend themselves against sexual guilt. Or perhaps they were precipitated by the patient's 'masturbation phantasies'. Indeed, Freud claimed early that July, hysteria and neurosis in general were due to defensively repressed and unconscious 'phantasies' or 'falsifications of memory' (Freud, 1892–1899, pp. 247, 258).

To this he added on 21 September 1897 the following four reasons for entirely abandoning his seduction or repressed abuse theory of hysteria:

> The continual disappointments in my attempts at bringing my analysis to a real conclusion, the running-away of people who had for a time seemed most in my grasp, the absence of the complete successes on which I had reckoned, the possibility of explaining the partial successes in other ways [...] Then came surprise at the fact that in every case the father, not excluding my own, had to be blamed as a pervert [...] Then, thirdly, the certain discovery that there are no indications of reality in the unconscious, so that one cannot distinguish between the truth and fiction that is cathected [invested] with affect [emotion]. [...] Fourthly, the reflection that in the most deep-going psychosis the unconscious memory does not break through, so that the secret of the childhood experiences is not betrayed even in the most confused delirium. (Freud, 1892–1899, pp. 259–260)

Many people have been, and remain appalled by Freud's rejection of his seduction theory claim that symptoms of hysteria and neurosis are due to sexual abuse of the patient when they were an infant or young child. Nor is this any surprise given the scale of such abuse as in the following report:

> According to the 2015–16 Crime Survey for England and Wales, 7% of people aged between 16 and 59 reported that they were sexually abused as a child. Although this survey did not include young children or all forms of sexual abuse, this still equates to over two million victims and survivors in that age bracket across England and Wales – a substantial proportion of the population. (Office for National Statistics, 2016, n.p.)

Perhaps some memories of sexual abuse in childhood are nevertheless the result of therapist suggestion, false memory syndrome, or of what is now diagnosed as Dissociative Identity Disorder (DID).

This, however, does not excuse the fact that, following his abandonment of his repressed abuse theory of hysteria, Freud paid little attention to ways other people, beginning with those who first look after us in our early childhood, shape our psychology. He did however recall during his self-analysis in autumn 1897 that the woman who looked after him until he was about two and a half years old, was 'his teacher in sexual matters' (Gay, 1988, p. 7).

Much better known in the history of psychoanalysis is Freud's self-analysis account of his own sexual feelings irrespective of what others might have said or done to him. They include his recalling in early October 1897 that his 'libido was stirred up towards *matrem* [his mother]' during the train journey taking them from Leipzig to Vienna when he was nearly four years old because he then had 'the opportunity' to see her naked (Freud, 1892–1899, pp. 261–262).

Following this memory Freud announced on 15 October 1897 his then newly minted theory that all young children sexually desire their mothers and are jealous on this account of their fathers. Linking this with the play *Oedipus Rex*, dramatizing Oedipus's unwitting murder of his father and marriage to his mother, Freud told his above-mentioned friend Fliess,

> I have found, in my own case too, falling in love with the mother and jealousy of the father, and I now regard it as a universal event of early childhood, even if not so early as in children who have been made hysterical. [...] If that is so, we can understand the riveting power of *Oedipus Rex* [...] [It] seizes on a compulsion which everyone recognizes because he feels its existence within himself. (Freud, 1892–1899, p. 265)

Freud thereby announced what became a major axiom of his foundation of psychoanalysis, namely the claim that, whether or not they are sexually abused as infants, all young children entertain the wishful fantasy of doing away with their father so as to realize sexual desire for their mother.

In early January 1899, however, Freud argued that such wishful fantasy may well be the product of psychological processes occurring long after infancy. Emphasizing the point to Fliess, he said,

> [A] small bit of my self-analysis has forced its way through, and confirmed that phantasies are products of later periods and are projected back from the then present on to the earliest childhood. (Freud, 1892–1899, p. 276)

Furthermore, he maintained, memories of early childhood must be the product of fantasy since researchers had shown that it is only from the age of five or six that we can recall memories as 'a connected chain of events' (Freud, 1899, p. 303).

He went on to provide a clear memory of just such a connected chain of events from his early childhood, a memory of which he said,

> I see a rectangular, rather steeply sloping piece of meadow-land, green and thickly grown; in the green there are a great number of yellow flowers – evidently common dandelions. At the top end of the meadow there is a cottage and in front of the cottage door two women are standing chatting busily, a peasant-woman with a

> handkerchief on her head and a children's nurse. Three children are playing in the grass. One of them is myself (between the age of two and three); the two others are my boy cousin, who is a year older than me, and his sister, who is almost exactly the same age as I am. We are picking the yellow flowers and each of us is holding a bunch of flowers we have already picked. The little girl has the best bunch; and, as though by mutual agreement, we – the two boys – fall on her and snatch away her flowers. (Freud, 1899, p. 311)

This memory occurred to Freud after he revisited his birthplace, Freiburg, when he was sixteen and stayed there with a family with whose teenage daughter, Gisela Fluss, he then fell in love. She features as the little girl in his above-recalled early childhood memory. It was after another event, however, occurring a few years later – namely his re-meeting his cousins (his half-brother Philipp's children with whom he used to play as a young child) – that this early childhood memory first occurred to Freud.

Why, though, its various details including himself and his boy cousin snatching Gisela's flowers? Because, Freud argued, this detail resulted from repressed unconscious desire as a sixteen-year-old to deflower or take Gisela's virginity away from her, this in the disguised conscious form of snatching her flowers.

Generalizing from this example, Freud concluded that memories of early childhood – he called them screen memories – result from subsequently occurring repressed and unconscious sexual wishes in the guise of consciously recalled recollections. Or as he put it,

> Our childhood memories show us our earliest years not as they were but as they appeared at the later periods when the memories were aroused. In these periods of arousal, the childhood memories did not, as people are accustomed to say, *emerge*; they were *formed* at that time. (Freud, 1899, p. 322, italics in original)

Such memories are the product of dynamic tension between what is unconscious and conscious.

SUMMARY: In September 1897, Freud abandoned his repressed abuse or seduction theory of hysteria. He went on to focus on wishful Oedipal fantasy occurring in early childhood, and on memories of early childhood as product of later occurring dynamic tension between repressed and unconscious sexual wishes and what is admissable to conscious recall.

CONCLUSIONS TO PART I

After doing research in physiology, anatomy, and into medical uses of cocaine, Freud specialized in the treatment of hysteria. Through his patients' resistance to hypnosis and his pressure technique, he formulated in 1895 the theory that their hysterical symptoms were due to repression and resulting unconsciousness of their sexual or erotic cause. In 1896, he formulated a repressed abuse or seduction theory of hysteria which he abandoned the following year in favour of emphasis on the role of repressed and unconscious sexual wishes fuelling fantasy-based memories of early childhood.

PART II
UNCONSCIOUS-CONSCIOUS DYNAMICS

Freud founds psychoanalysis in 1900 with his book *The Interpretation of Dreams*. In it he announces his revolutionary account of the repressed unconscious and its contribution, in more or less disguised form, to our consciously recalled dreams. Freud follows this with an account of similar unconscious-conscious dynamics operating in what we now describe as Freudian slips of the tongue. He also writes about jokes. In 1905, he adds a revolutionary account of psychological development in terms of oral, anal, and genital stages followed by latency in middle childhood, the revival with puberty of our earliest sexual attachment to the person who first mothered us, and observations regarding the incest taboo.

DREAMS

Often regarded as marking the start of Freud's revolutionary transformation of psychology with his theory of what is repressed and unconscious, his 1900 book, *The Interpretation of Dreams*, begins with previous age-old approaches to interpreting dreams. These approaches include attributing them to the work of gods, demons, or other external forces.

Dreams have also been explained, not least by some neuroscientists today, as meaningless product of neurological processes in the brain. In keeping with this viewpoint, some people argue that seeing meaning in dreams is akin to seeing meaning in tea leaves, doodles, or inkblots. It might be a fun pastime. But it tells us nothing of any importance about the dreamer's psychology.

In contrast to this dismissive attitude to dreams, their interpretation has often been regarded as a worthwhile activity. It has, for instance, been regarded as a useful means of predicting the future. A well-known example is Joseph in the Old Testament (and in the musical *Joseph and the Amazing Technicolour Dreamcoat*), who interpreted a pharaoh's dream of seven fat cows and seven lean cows as meaning that there would be seven years of good harvest and seven years of bad harvest. Armed with this prediction, it was thought worthwhile to store grain from the good harvest years ready for when the harvest was bad.

Using dreams to predict the future is not confined to the Old Testament. Many others have understood dreams in these terms. They include Freud's one-time psychoanalytic colleague Carl Gustav Jung. Following the end of their friendship Jung provided various examples of the predictive use of dreams. They included the example of an older medical colleague of whom Jung said,

> He had dreamed [...] 'I am climbing a high mountain over steep, snow-covered slopes. I mount higher and higher – it is marvellous weather. The higher I climb, the better I feel. I think: "If only I could go on climbing like this for ever!" When I reach the summit, my happiness and elation are so strong that I feel I could mount right up into space. And I discover that I actually can do this. I go on climbing on empty air. I awake in a real ecstasy'. [...] Three months after this [...] [h]e went on a climb [...] without guides. An alpinist standing below saw him literally step out into the air as he was letting himself down a rock wall. He fell on to the head of his friend, who was waiting beneath him, and both were dashed to pieces far below. (Jung, 1933, pp. 17–18)

If only he had paid more attention to his dream foretelling his fateful stepping out into air, Jung indicated, this man's life might not have thus been brought short.

Jung also interpreted dreams in terms of symbols representing what he described as archetypes of the collective unconscious. We too can do something similar by using a dictionary of dream symbols, such as the 2017 book *The Dream Interpretation Dictionary: Symbols, Signs and Meanings*, to discover the meaning of parts of our dreams or of our dreams as a whole.

Freud adopted a different method for interpreting dreams. In his psychoanalytic practice he sought to discover the origin of his patients' symptoms by pressing them to recall whatever occurred in association to them (see p. 13 above). He adopted a similar free association method in interpreting dreams. He pressed himself, his relatives, his patients, and friends to recall whatever occurred to them in association to bits and pieces of their dreams. In justifying this piecemeal method, he wrote,

> If I say to a patient who is still a novice: 'What occurs to you in connection with this dream?', as a rule his mental horizon becomes a blank. If, however, I put the dream before him cut up into pieces, he will give me a series of associations to each piece, which might be described as 'background thoughts' of that particular part of the dream. (Freud, 1900, pp. 103–104)

Examples of Freud's free association method can be found in his interpretation of a dream which he had on the night of 23/24 July 1895 and which involved a patient, Irma, his pseudonym for his patient Emma Eckstein (referred to on p. 17 above). To illustrate Freud's free association method of dream interpretation, I have selected the following fragment from this dream:

> A large hall – numerous guests, whom we were receiving – among them was Irma [...] I said to her: If you still get pains it's really your own fault! [...] I took her to the window and looked down her throat [...] on the right I found a big white patch [...] Not long before, when she was feeling unwell, my friend Otto had given her an injection of a preparation of [...] propionic acid [...] probably the syringe had not been clean. (Freud, 1900, p. 107)

Free associating to 'a big white patch' in this dream fragment, Freud recalled the serious illness of his oldest daughter, Mathilde. On the basis of this and other associations to bits of this dream, he interpreted it as fulfilling his 'wish to be innocent' of Irma's illness. Generalizing from this and other dream examples, he concluded that '[w]hen the work of interpretation has been completed, we perceive that a dream is the fulfilment of a wish' (Freud, 1900, pp. 111, 120, 121).

Sometimes, he pointed out, the wish fulfilled by a dream is obvious. Examples for Freud included a dream of his eighteen-month-old daughter, Anna, of which he said in October 1897

> She had to starve one day at Aussee [some distance from Vienna] because she was sick in the morning, which was put down to a meal of strawberries. During the following night she called out a whole menu in her sleep: 'Stawbewwies, wild stwawbewwies, omblet, pudden!' (Freud, 1892–1899, p. 267).

From these words, shouted out as she slept, Freud concluded they signified the wished for food Anna dreamt she was having as she slept.

Another example for Freud of a wish-fulfilling dream involved a young man, Pepi, of whom he recalled,

> One morning sleep seemed peculiarly sweet. [His] landlady called through the door: 'Wake up, Herr Pepi! it's time to go to the hospital!' In response to this [Pepi] had a dream that he was lying in bed in a room in the hospital, and that there was a card over the bed on which was written: 'Pepi H., medical student, age 22'. While he was dreaming, he said to himself 'As I'm already *in* the hospital, there's no need for me to go there' – and turned over and went on sleeping. (Freud, 1900, p. 125, italics in original)

Whereas this dream was triggered by an external stimulus – Pepi's landlady calling out for him to wake up – other dreams are triggered by an internal stimulus. Examples include Freud feeling hungry and dreaming, 'I went into a kitchen in search of some pudding' (Freud, 1900, p. 204).

Thoughts from the previous day can also act as an internal stimulus for a dream. Among several examples Freud recalled one in which he dreamt, 'I took out a subscription in S. and R.'s bookshop for a periodical costing twenty florins a year'. The day before, he said, in recalling the stimulus for this dream, his wife had reminded him that he still 'owed her twenty florins for the weekly household expenses' (Freud, 1900, p. 166).

How, though, does such a stimulus result in a dream? In answering this question Freud argued that the stimulus provokes an unconscious wish. He likened the stimulus and unconscious wish respectively to an entrepreneur and a capitalist, of whom he said,

> [T]he *entrepreneur*, who, as people say, has the idea and the initiative to carry it out, can do nothing without capital; he needs a *capitalist* who can afford the outlay, and the capitalist who provides the psychical outlay for the dream is invariably and indisputably, whatever may be the thoughts of the previous day, *a wish from the unconscious*. (Freud, 1900, p. 561, italics in original)

This analogy has since been recast in neuroscience terms by the psychoanalyst Mark Solms and the neuropsychologist Oliver Turnbull (2002). They argue that dreams result from an internal or external stimulus occurring during sleep bypassing the frontal lobe of the brain and triggering the junction of nerves from the brain's parietal, occipital, and temporal lobes (diagrammed below). As a result, this stimulus evokes sensory, visual, memory-based, and other aspects of the hallucination we recall as a dream.

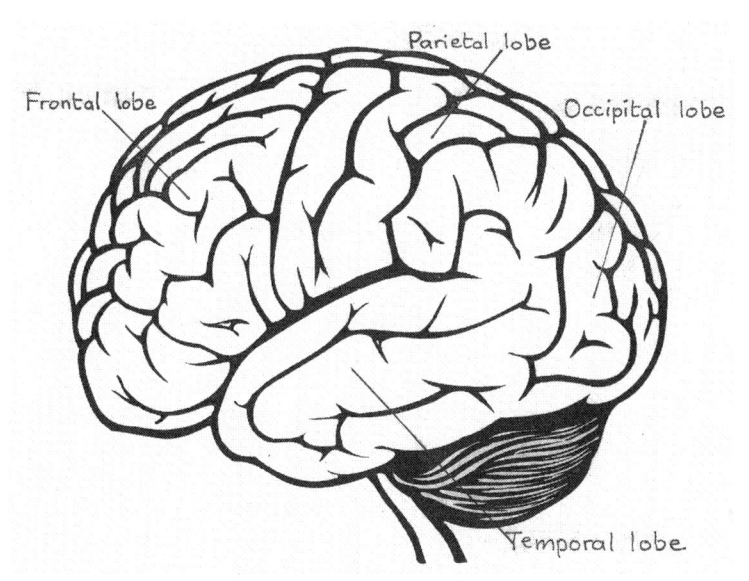

Figure 6.1 Brain lobes diagram

But what if the hallucination or dream wakes the sleeper, thereby preventing fulfilment of the unconscious wish fuelling it? To stop this happening, argued Freud, and to enable albeit hallucinatory dream fulfilment of the unconscious wish fuelling the dream, the 'latent content' of this wish is subjected to various forms of dream-work disguise or repression (Freud, 1900, p. 174).

One form of dream-work disguise is condensation. It involves representing several people, things, or ideas in the latent or unconscious dream-thoughts by a single element in the manifest dream recalled on waking. An example of this form of dream-work disguise occurred in a dream I had about a man called Albert. It turned out that with this man I had condensed two people together: my French teacher, Albert, at school; and the well-known physicist Albert Einstein.

A second dream-work disguise is displacement. It involves shifting a psychologically significant element of the dream onto a relatively insignificant detail. Examples for Freud included a woman patient who said of a dream,

> She called to mind that she had two may-beetles in a box and that she must set them free or they would suffocate. She opened the box and the may-beetles were in an exhausted state. One of them flew out of the open window; but the other was crushed by the casement while she was shutting it at someone's request. (Freud, 1900, p. 289)

This dream involved the patient shifting a significant item in the dream – a crushed beetle which she knew to be a powerful aphrodisiac or stimulant of sexual desire – to a virtual afterthought at the end of this her remembered dream.

For Freud a third form of dream-work disguise uses the visual or other form of representation in which dreams manifest themselves. This can involve disguising the dream's underlying wishful cause in terms of vagueness, ambiguity, or absurdity. An example of vagueness was one of Freud's dreams of which he told Fliess in April 1897, 'It was a telegraph message about your whereabouts [in Venice]'. The dream left vague whether Fliess's whereabouts – his address – involved the words 'Via', 'Villa', or 'Casa'. Why this ambiguity? Because, said

Freud, he was angry with Fliess for staying at this address rather than at 'Casa Kirsch' where he had recommended him to stay (Freud, 1892–1899, p. 245).

A fourth and last dream-work disguise identified by Freud is the process whereby, in recalling our dreams as a story or narrative whole, we iron out irregularities and oddities which might lead us to discover the unconscious wishes they fulfil. Hence the value of Freud's method of free association to bits and pieces of dreams. It serves as a way of undoing the secondary revision, story-like disguise, of our dreams' unconscious wish-fulfilling meaning.

Unfortunately, however, there are problems with Freud's free association method for discovering the unconscious wishes which he claimed our dreams fulfil. This method is based on the assumption that dreams are not just the meaningless effect of neurological processes in the brain. It assumes that dreams are meaningful. It cannot therefore be used to test the validity of this assumption.

Another problem is the fact that the associations the dreamer produces might well be influenced by their theories about dreams or, if they are in psychoanalytic treatment, by the theories of their psychoanalyst. Furthermore, whatever the dreamer recalls in association to their dream, might not have caused it. To assume otherwise is to commit the fallacy of *post hoc ergo propter hoc*, the fallacy, in the case of dreams, that because a free association occurred after a dream, this dream occurred because of what was recalled in this association.

There is also the self-fulfilling prophecy problem. Freud's claim that every dream involves a more or less disguised wish fulfilment can result in this claim being fulfilled through the dreamer going on free associating to elements of their dream, even if it is a nightmare, until they arrive at a possible wish-fulfilling cause.

Despite these problems Freud forged an intriguing theory regarding the origin in early infancy of the wish-fulfilling character of dreams. He explained this aspect of dreams in terms of the infant's early psychological development. In particular he argued that the wish-fulfilling character of dreams begins in early child development with the hungry baby hallucinating the perception involved in its previous experience of its hunger being reduced. If it is a breast-fed baby, it hallucinates itself sucking at the breast.

Freud described this as the developmentally earliest 'primary process' form of wish-fulfilling unconscious thinking. He contrasted it with its inhibition by reality-oriented 'secondary process' conscious thinking (Freud, 1900, p. 601). That said, he famously concluded,

> The interpretation of dreams is the royal road to a knowledge of the unconscious activities of the mind. (Freud, 1900, pp. 601, 608)

These unconscious, primary process activities are, he indicated, in dynamic tension with, and inhibited by, or repressed in favour of the activities of the secondary process conscious mind. He began developing this revolutionary theory of what is repressed and unconscious in his 'Project for a scientific psychology' (Freud, 1895a). He further explained it in a brief article, 'Formulations on the two principles of mental functioning' (Freud, 1911a).

SUMMARY: Freud interpreted dreams as motivated by unconscious wish-fulfilling latent thoughts. If they risk waking the dreamer, they are subject, he said, to dream-work repressive disguise. This can be undone, he argued, through the dreamer free associating to bits and pieces of the manifest dream they recall on waking. Although Freud's free association method has problems, his use of this method led him to conclude that dreams result from an unconscious primary process of mind inhibited and repressed by, and in dynamic tension with, secondary process conscious thinking.

FREUDIAN SLIPS

Having described the dynamic interplay in dreams between unconscious and conscious, primary and secondary processes of the mind, Freud turned to a similar dynamic operating in everyday errors, now widely known as Freudian slips. So basic are these slips to the legacy bequeathed by Freud, he has been pictured in terms of them, as in the following image.

For Freud, instances of everyday slips and errors included the forgetting of names when, he observed, alternative possible names often come to mind. He illustrated this with the example of his forgetting the name of the artist who painted the Capella Nuova frescoes in the cathedral of the Italian town Orvieto. Unable to recall this artist's name, two other artists' names occurred to Freud – Botticelli and Boltraffio. Why? Because, he said, both names begin with 'Bo' as does 'Bosnia' – a place he was discussing with a travelling companion just before he forgot the Orvieto artist's name.

He had also been telling this companion a story he had heard from a doctor working in Bosnia–Herzegovina. It involved Turkish peasants saying, with respect to loss of sexual potency, 'Herr [Sir], you must know that if *that* comes to an end then life is of no value' (Freud, 1901b, p. 3, italics in original).

FREUDIAN SLIP

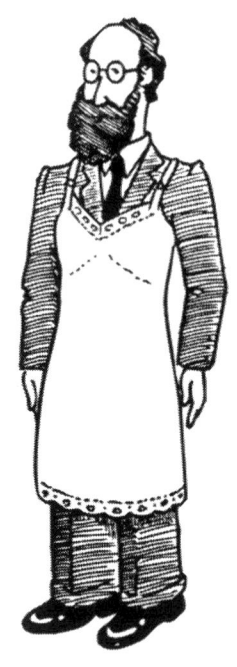

Figure 7.1 Freudian slip
Mike Monahan/Shutterstock.com

This reminded Freud that, while staying at Trafoi, in the Italian Tyrol, he had learnt that one of his patients had committed suicide due to an incurable sexual disorder. Armed with this reminder, Freud understood the unconscious cause of his forgetting the name of the painter of the Capella Nuova frescoes. His name was Signorelli.

'Signor' – or rather 'Herr' – figures in the name of the country Bosnia–Herzegovina, about which Freud and his travelling companion had talked before Freud forgot the name Signorelli. Furthermore 'Herr' is akin in meaning to 'Signor' in Signorelli. And the name Signorelli includes the 'elli' of 'Botticelli', which occurred to Freud in place of Signorelli's name. Moreover 'Trafoi' is not unlike the second two syllables of 'Boltraffio', which also occurred to Freud when he could not remember Signorelli's name.

This is not altogether convincing as an account of the unconscious–conscious dynamic involved in forgetting names. It reads more like an explanation of the answer to a cryptic crossword clue than as substantial evidence for the repressed unconscious cause of this type of Freudian slip. Freud nevertheless concluded from this and similar examples that such forgetting is almost always 'motivated by repression' (Freud, 1901b, p. 7).

Further everyday slips or errors included for Freud the forgetting of foreign words. Why, he asked himself, did one of his acquaintances forget the word *aliquis* in the Latin phrase 'Exoriare aliquis nostris ex ossibus ultor' ('Let someone arise as an avenger from my bones')? After Freud provided this acquaintance with the forgotten word – *aliquis* – and after he also persuaded him to free associate to this word, this acquaintance recalled the words 'liquefying', 'fluidity', and 'fluid'. They reminded him of something he wanted to repress and forget, namely the fact that his girlfriend had missed her period and might be pregnant (Freud, 1901b, p. 9).

Sometimes the reason we repress and forget a particular name is very obvious. The following is a case in point.

> A Herr Y. fell in love with a lady; but he met with no success, and shortly afterwards she married a Herr X. Thereafter, Herr Y., in spite of having known Herr X. for a long time and even having business dealings with him, forgot his name over and over again, so that several times he had to enquire what it was from other people when he wanted to correspond with Herr X. (Freud, 1901b, p. 25)

To these and other more or less unconsciously motivated forgetting of names Freud added more or less unconsciously motivated misremembered scenes from early childhood. They included his screen memory involving Gisela Fluss (see p. 24 above). Another example of misremembering involved a recollection of himself aged two, a recollection of which he said,

> I saw myself standing in front of a cupboard [*Kasten*] demanding something and screaming, while my half-brother [Philipp] [...] held it open. Then suddenly my mother, looking beautiful and slim, walked into the room, as if she had come in from the street. (Freud, 1901b, p. 50)

Freud's self-analysis revealed that this misremembered scene was related to Philipp saying of Freud's nursemaid when he was two and his mother was absent, giving birth to his sister, Anna, that she had been 'boxed up' or *eingekastelt*, meaning 'put in a *Kasten* or cupboard'. It was, said Freud, because he suspected that his mother's absence was due to Philipp having boxed her up in a cupboard that he saw himself, aged two, in this misremembered scene forcing Philipp to open a cupboard.

From misremembered childhood incidents Freud turned to other errors or parapraxes, as his English translator called them. They included slips of the tongue involving the substitution of one word for another. Freud gave the example of the president of an Austrian house of parliament opening one of its sessions by saying: 'Gentlemen: I take notice that a full quorum of members is present and herewith declare the sitting *closed*!' Such slips nicely reveal to witnesses and also perhaps to the speaker the latter's more or less repressed unconscious wishes. Further examples provided by Freud include a young woman who in describing the diet recommended by the doctor for her ailing husband said, 'He can eat and drink what *I* want' (Freud, 1901b, pp. 59, 70, italics in the original).

Slips of the tongue can also occur due to unconscious identification of one person with another. Freud illustrated this with the examples of a patient repeatedly referring to his aunt as his mother, and someone else repeatedly referring to her husband as her brother. Similar more or less unconscious identification of one person with another doubtless underlies examples today of young children at school calling their teacher 'Mummy'.

Other Freudian slips involve miswriting. Examples for Freud included one which he added to his book *The Psychopathology of Everyday Life*, after the 1914–1918 World War. It involved a man who, having separated on rather bad terms from his wife in America, invited her to join him in Europe. In his resulting letter he wrote, 'It would be fine if you could come on the *Lusitania* as I did'. Then, remembering that the *Lusitania* had famously been sunk in 1915 by a German submarine during the war, he crossed out the word 'Lusitania'. Not wanting his wife to see that he had mistakenly suggested she come on this sunken ship, he replaced this letter with another one in which he invited her to come on the intact *Mauretania*.

Another instance of an unhappy marriage was used by Freud to illustrate unconsciously motivated 'bungled actions' (Freud, 1901b, p. 162). It involved a young woman who, while staying with her very jealous husband at the home of her married sister, showed off her ability as a cancan dancer to much applause. Her husband, however, derided her dancing as behaving like a prostitute. His derision left her feeling so nervous that when, the following day, 'the horses bolted' when she was in the carriage which they were pulling, 'she took the opportunity of jumping out the carriage and breaking her leg' (Freud, 1892–1899, p. 246). It was, said Freud, an unconsciously motivated 'punishment' making it 'impossible for her to dance the can-can for quite a long time' (Freud, 1901b, p. 180).

A striking example for Freud of another unconsciously motivated mistake involved a young woman who, while shopping with her sister, noticed a man on the other side of the street. 'Look, there goes Herr L.', she said, not remembering that Herr L. was her husband with whom she had just been on honeymoon. No surprise, commented Freud, the marriage had 'a most unhappy end' (Freud, 1901b, p. 203).

Other instances of slips or bungled actions involve missed appointments. Those they affect can readily recognize their unconscious cause. Reading this observation by Freud reminded me of an incident when I arrived at a different station in London from the one where I had agreed to meet a friend. She had no difficulty in recognizing its unconscious motive – my not wanting to meet her.

Freud's account of another slip – unconsciously motivated mislaying of things – reminded me of another incident. For many months I mislaid and could not find an address book. I only found it after I no longer had a repressed unconscious reason, it seems, for not doing so.

Further examples of Freudian slips include the following story told by the mother of four children:

> Remembering her pregnancy with her fourth child, she recalled that during this pregnancy she worried that the baby might not be okay. The relevant medical test was reassuring. She was nevertheless offered a further test. By then, however, she said, she was twenty-four months into her pregnancy. So she decided to go through with it. Twenty-four months! Surely this was a Freudian slip. By twenty-four months the baby would have been well and truly born. Maybe her slip served to indicate her having resolved conflict between an unconscious wish to end her pregnancy with this child, and conscious relief that she had not done so.

Britain's Brexit controversy spawned many more Freudian slips. They included a presenter on early morning radio saying, 'The Labour party won the Peterborough by-election despite a strong challenge from Nigel Farrage's breakfast – no, Brexit – party'; and a television presenter during particularly stormy Brexit agitation referring to the political commentator Robert Peston, as Robert Pester.

SUMMARY: After developing his theory regarding the dynamic interplay of the unconscious and conscious mind involved in dreams, Freud illustrated a similar dynamic operating in what have come to be known as Freudian slips.

JOKES

As well as finding evidence of dynamic interplay between the unconscious and conscious mind in dreams and in everyday slips and errors, Freud also found evidence of this interplay in jokes. Or, rather, he provided evidence of jokes involving similar dream-work mechanisms to those involved in transforming an unconscious wish into a consciously remembered dream.

An example for Freud of a joke relying on the dream-work mechanism of condensation involved one in which two words – 'familiarly' and 'millionaire' – were condensed together into a single word. In this joke a man boasted about his close involvement with the millionaire Rothschild family by saying, 'I sat beside Salomon Rothschild and he treated me quite as his equal – quite famillionairely' (Freud, 1905d, p. 16).

Another example for Freud of condensation in jokes was someone criticizing a celebrity by saying, '[H]e has a great future behind him'. After all, Freud explained, this joke condenses two ideas that can be expressed by two clauses in the sentence, 'The man has had a great future before him, but he has it no longer' (Freud, 1905d, p. 26).

And, of course, condensation is also involved in jokes involving the *double entendres*, or double meanings, involved in punning – a form of humour regarded by Freud with 'contempt' (Freud, 1905d, p. 45). Christmas cracker jokes are notorious in this respect. Recent examples include the following:

> Why couldn't the skeleton go to the Christmas party? He had no body to go with.
> Where does Santa go when he's sick? To an elf centre.
> What do reindeer hang on their Christmas trees? Horn-aments!

Other forms of condensation occur in risqué sexual humour of which Freud particularly liked the following example:

> Some people think that the husband has earned a lot and so has been able to lay by a bit [*sich etwas zurückgelegt*]; others again think that the wife has lain back a bit [*sich etwas zurückgelegt*] and so has been able to earn a lot. (Freud, 1905d, p. 40)

Perhaps this would be funnier if one were more familiar with the double meaning of the German phrase on which this joke depends.

Not only is the dream-work process of condensation involved in joke-work. So too, according to Freud, is the dream-work mechanism of displacement. An instance for him was the following:

> Two Jews met in the neighbourhood of the bath-house. 'Have you taken a bath?' asked one of them. 'What?' asked the other in return, 'is there one missing?' (Freud, 1905d, p. 49)

This joke works, said Freud, through displacing emphasis by the first speaker on 'bath' onto the word 'taken' in the second speaker's question.

A yet further dream-work mechanism involved in jokes, argued Freud, is representation using ambiguity, nonsense, and other disguises of a dream's unconscious meaning. Examples of similar dream- or joke-work disguises included for Freud an Irish joke of which he said,

> A guide was conducting a company of old and young visitors from figure to figure [in a wax-work museum] and commenting on them: 'This is the Duke of Wellington and his horse', he explained. Whereupon a young lady asked: 'Which is the Duke of Wellington and which is his horse?' 'Just as you like, my pretty child', was the reply. 'You pays your money and you takes your choice'. (Freud, 1905d, p. 71)

Why, though, is this amusing? Because, Freud explained,

> In place of the public in general an individual lady appears and the figure of the rider is particularized: he must be the Duke of Wellington, who is so extremely popular in Ireland. But the shamelessness of the proprietor or guide, who takes money out of people's pockets and offers them nothing in return, is represented by the opposite – by a speech in which he boasts himself a conscientious man of business, who has nothing more closely at heart than regard for the rights which the public has acquired by its payment. (Freud, 1905d, p. 71)

From similarities between the dream-work mechanisms of condensation, displacement, and representation transforming unconscious wish fulfilment into a consciously remembered dream and the same mechanisms involved in what he described as joke-work, Freud turned to the contrast between 'innocent' and 'tendentious' jokes. The latter, he argued, involve at least three people: the person who makes the joke; the person who is the object of its hostile or sexual aggression; and the person whose 'lustful' or 'hostile' instinctual pleasure the joke is designed to evoke (Freud, 1905d, pp. 90, 101).

Such jokes are made acceptable, he maintained, through their lustful or hostile content being disguised or repressed just as similar content is repressed in our consciously recalled dreams. Examples of tendentious jokes included for Freud the disguised hostility directed against the bride, bridegroom, and their parents in Jewish marriage broker jokes. Instances abound in Freud's jokes book, of which the following is an illustrative example

> The bridegroom was most disagreeably surprised when the bride was introduced to him, and drew the broker on one side and whispered his remonstrances: 'Why have you brought me here?' he asked reproachfully. 'She's ugly and old, she squints and has bad teeth and bleary eyes ...' – 'You needn't lower your voice', interrupted the broker, 'she's deaf as well'. (Freud, 1905d, p. 64, ellipses in the original)

Other examples of Jewish marriage broker jokes, cited by Freud, similarly rely on blatant misogyny making one feel uneasy.

Having previously likened jokes to dreams – at least in terms of the latter's dream-work construction – Freud went on to note in his jokes book ways in which jokes differ from dreams. After all, he pointed out, we require jokes, unlike dreams, to be intelligible to those to whom they are told.

And, of course, we require jokes, unlike dreams, to be funny. Many of the jokes Freud tells in his jokes book are indeed very funny. Unfortunately, however, several of the jokes he relates do not translate readily from German into English. As a result, they are not very amusing for those not well versed in German. Perhaps that is why Freud's jokes book is not mentioned in the otherwise very full and detailed account of his life provided by his biographers, Peter Gay (1988) and Elisabeth Roudinesco (2016).

> *SUMMARY:* In his account of jokes Freud provided examples of ways in which their more or less unconscious meaning is disguised by mechanisms similar to those involved in disguising unconscious wishes in our consciously remembered dreams. He also provided examples of the repression of lustful or hostile material in what he described as tendentious jokes.

SEX

After writing books about dreams, everyday errors (now known as Freudian slips), and jokes, Freud wrote his 1905 book, *Three Essays on the Theory of Sexuality*. Beginning with sexual perversions and the role of sexuality in hysteria and neurosis, he went on in this book to forge a revolutionary account of developmental psychology in terms of oral, anal, and genital precursors in infancy and early childhood of adult psychology.

SEXUAL PERVERSIONS

'Popular opinion has quite definite ideas about the nature and characteristics of this sexual instinct', Freud announced at the start of this book.

> [The sexual instinct] is generally understood to be absent in childhood, to set in at the time of puberty in connection with the process of coming to maturity and to be revealed in the manifestations of an irresistible attraction exercised by one sex upon the other; while its aim is presumed to be sexual union, or at all events actions leading in that direction. (Freud, 1905b, p. 135)

Yet, he pointed out, sexual perversions indicate that the object and aim of the sexual instinct can vary considerably from popular ideas about it.

In his 1886 book, *Psychopathia Sexualis*, the psychiatrist Richard Krafft-Ebing had provided a detailed catalogue of sexual perversions. Now, in 1905, Freud argued that sexual perversions indicate that the object of the sexual instinct can vary. It can be someone of the same or the opposite sex to oneself. It can be an adult, child, or animal who is alive or dead. Or it can be part of someone or something else. These variations convinced Freud that the object of the sexual instinct is not fixed like the object – food and drink – of the instincts of hunger and thirst.

Evidence from sexual perversions – oral and anal sex, for instance – indicated to Freud that the aim as well as the object of the sexual instinct can vary. Its aim can, for instance, be oral, anal, or genital. Furthermore the perversions of sadism and masochism, and of voyeurism and exhibitionism indicated to Freud that the sexual instinct can express itself in active or passive form.

Having in effect defined non-perverse sex as aimed at heterosexual genital union, Freud argued that 'the less severe perversions' – the oral pleasure of kissing, for instance – 'are rarely absent from the sexual life of healthy people' (Freud, 1905b, p. 160). To this he added the observation that his clinical work had shown him the roots of neurosis in the early 'sexual life' of the patient (Freud, 1905b, pp. 160, 163). That said, he went on to describe oral, anal, genital, and subsequent stages of psychosexual development.

ORAL STAGE

Freud illustrated the first oral stage of infant sexuality with the example of thumbsucking, of which he said,

> [It] is determined by a search for some pleasure which has already been experienced and is now remembered. In the simplest case [the infant] proceeds to find this satisfaction by sucking rhythmically at some part of the skin or mucous membrane. It is easy to guess the occasions on which the child had his first experiences of the pleasure

> which he is now striving to renew. It was the child's first and most vital activity, his sucking at his mother's breast, or at substitutes for it, that must have familiarized him with this pleasure. (Freud, 1905b, p. 181)

But does the oral pleasure of thumbsucking begin with breast- or bottle feeding? Not so, according to recent research which indicates that babies suck their thumbs in the womb (see e.g. Chalk, 2013).

That aside, thumbsucking was regarded in Freud's time as an aspect of the 'sexual "naughtiness" of children' (Freud, 1905b, p. 180). It was, and still is often curbed and frowned on if it persists too long. In my own case, despite attempts by my relatives to stop me doing it, my thumbsucking continued for so long it has left me with one thumb almost a centimetre shorter than the other.

So prevalent is thumbsucking in early infancy, it features in many cartoons. Examples include the infant Linus in the following image from the comic strip *Peanuts*. Noting ways in which infants often accompany their thumbsucking with the pleasurable sensation of cuddling a blanket, as in this example, the psychoanalyst Donald

Figure 9.1 PEANUTS © Peanuts Worldwide LLC. Dist.
By Andrews McMeel Syndication.
Reprinted with permission. All rights reserved.

Winnicott (1951) argued that such objects serve as a transitional bridge between the infant and its mother or other primary caregiver.

ANAL STAGE

In addition to postulating the existence of an oral stage in infant psychosexual development, Freud postulated an anal stage beginning when the infant gains control of its urinary and anal sphincters. Evidence of the sensual pleasure infants derive from this form of control included for Freud the fact that

> [They hold] back their stool till its accumulation brings about violent muscular contractions and, as it passes through the anus, is able to produce powerful stimulation of the mucous membrane. In so doing it must no doubt cause not only painful but also highly pleasurable sensations. (Freud, 1905b, p. 186)

Infants, he pointed out, clearly value their faeces as a 'gift' (Freud, 1905b, p. 186). They are a 'surprise', a little girl told me, 'like presents at Christmas'. But, as the psychoanalyst Marion Milner pointed out, infants also learn that, to others, their 'anal mess' is 'not literally as lovely as the feelings experienced in making it' (Milner, 1955, p. 122).

Nevertheless it may well feel very lovely to the infant itself. This was evidently true of the two-year-old boy in the following example:

> After being put in his cot for an afternoon nap, his mother returned some time later to discover that, in her absence, he had used a wide paint brush together with pooh from his nappy to daub the wall beside his cot. Doubtless he enjoyed the experience. Not so his mother on seeing and smelling the result.

As this example illustrates, parents and others are not necessarily delighted by infant manifestations of anal pleasure – this doubtless contributing to infant, and subsequent, pleasure in the naughtiness of lavatorial humour. Anal pleasure or preoccupation may also contribute to infants understanding childbirth in anal terms.

GENITAL STAGE

As well as postulating oral and anal stages in psychosexual stages Freud postulated a genital stage. In doing so he maintained that for the boy this stage includes the assumption that, like him, girls have a penis. Boys only abandon this assumption 'after severe internal struggles', Freud argued in describing these struggles as constituting the boy's 'castration complex'. Furthermore, he maintained, 'substitutes' for the penis in women 'play a great part in determining the form taken by many perversions', while girls, he notoriously added, no sooner see the penis of boys than they suffer with 'penis envy', this culminating in the wish 'to be boys themselves' (Freud, 1905b, p. 195).

LATENCY

Why do we not remember these aspects of our early psychological development? Because, said Freud, they are subject to 'infantile amnesia' as a result of 'disgust, feelings of shame and the claims of aesthetic and moral ideals'. These feelings usher in, he added, a period of sexual 'latency' in middle childhood whereby the sexual aims of infancy are diverted by 'sublimation' into 'cultural achievement' (Freud, 1905b, pp. 177, 178).

PUBERTY

With puberty comes the capacity for genital orgasm. It results, or should result, Freud claimed, in subordination of the oral and anal 'erotogenetic' zones to genital pleasure (Freud, 1905b, p. 211). For girls, he insisted, this subordination entails transfer of sexual pleasure from the clitoris to the vagina – a claim ridiculed by many of his critics, not least Anne Koedt (1970), who described it as perpetrating a myth of the vaginal orgasm.

More widely accepted is Freud's argument that in choosing a sexual partner or 'object', as he put it, we are mindful of the person who first aroused our sexual desire in earliest infancy, namely the person who first mothered us. He accordingly maintained that 'a child sucking at his mother's breast has become the prototype of every relation of love' such that '[t]he finding of an object is in fact a refinding of it' (Freud, 1905b, p. 222).

It is through our mothers that, as infants and young children, we, first learn to love. Hence, Freud argued, loss of the mother causes anxiety. It is for this reason, he claimed, that the adult who becomes neurotic and frightened when 'he is alone' and 'away from someone of whose love he had felt secure' seeks to comfort themselves with 'childish measures' (Freud, 1905b, p. 224).

INCEST TABOO

'No doubt the simplest course for the child would be to choose as his sexual objects the same persons whom, since his childhood, he has loved', Freud observed. But to do so would contravene 'the barrier against incest' (Freud, 1905b, p. 225).

Why this barrier, highlighted by Freud, which is often referred to as the incest taboo? Not because incest keeps 'bad' genes in the gene pool, thereby compounding their effects such that closely related parents are likely to have offspring with reduced chances of survival (Mosher, 2008, n.p.). Rather, said Freud, explaining the barrier against incest,

> Society must defend itself against the danger that the interests which it needs for the establishment of higher social units may be swallowed up by the family; and for this reason, in the case of every individual, but in particular of adolescent boys, it seeks by all possible means to loosen their connection with their family – a connection which, in their childhood, is the only important one. (Freud, 1905b, p. 225)

Nevertheless, he concluded, 'unhappy experience in love' can result in neurotic regression to 'infantile fondness' for those, usually our close relatives, who first evoke our love (Freud, 1905b, p. 228).

> *SUMMARY:* With his 1905 book about sex Freud drew on evidence from sexual perversions and from his clinical work with neurotic patients in revolutionizing developmental psychology. He did this by describing its oral, anal, and genital aspects in infancy and early childhood and their repercussions, together with the incest taboo, on the psychology of puberty and beyond.

- Freud introduced the idea of developmental stages in childhood (although not sure about the content).
- He talked about taboo - sex.
- That childhood adversity can effect adulthood.

CONCLUSIONS TO PART II

With books published between 1900 and 1905, Freud founded the basic tenets of psychoanalysis. They included his revolutionary account of repressed and unconscious wish-fulfilling aspects of the unconscious mind evident from free associations to, and the interpretation of consciously remembered dreams. To this he added examples of unconscious-conscious dynamics in everyday errors or slips and jokes; as well as a revolutionary perspective on oral, anal, and genital precursors in infancy and early childhood of the individual's subsequent psychological development.

PART III
PSYCHOANALYTIC CASE STUDIES

Freud develops psychoanalysis in terms of five long case studies. They begin in 1905 with his study of an eighteen-year-old patient, Dora. Through this study Freud highlights the value of dreams in psychoanalytic treatment and the importance of psychoanalysts paying attention to ways patients transfer onto them their more or less unconscious experience of other significant people in their lives. In the second 1909 case study, Freud highlights with the example of a four-year-old patient, Hans, the patient's displacement of fear for and of his father onto a phobia of horses. This is followed by a third case study, also published in 1909, in which Freud recounts his psychoanalytic treatment of a young man, Ernst Lanzer's rat punishment obsession in terms of conflict in Lanzer between repressed and unconscious hatred and conscious love of his father. Freud's fourth long case study, published in 1911, documents his psychoanalytic understanding of a judge, Daniel Paul Schreber's published account of his schizophrenia. Fifth and last, Freud psychoanalyses the early childhood nightmare of a Russian patient, Sergei Pankejeff, in explaining the Oedipus and the castration complex cause of Pankejeff's anxiety and nervous symptoms when he was four.

DORA'S DREAMS

In his first long psychoanalytic case study Freud focused on an eighteen-year-old patient, Ida Bauer, whom he referred to as Dora. Her treatment with him began in October 1900 after her parents discovered a suicide note she had written, and after an argument with her father which culminated in what Freud described as Dora's hysterical loss of consciousness, convulsions, and delirium.

Her symptoms of hysteria also included a nervous cough and depression. They began following an incident when she was sexually propositioned, aged fifteen or sixteen, by a family friend, Herr K, on a walk by a lake near the home where she and her father were then staying with him and his family. After he emphatically denied that he had sexually propositioned her, Dora repeatedly pressed her father to break off all friendship with the K family.

Herr K's sexual proposition to Dora had not come entirely out of the blue. Previously he had engineered to get her, when she was thirteen or fourteen years old, to meet him alone at his office where he clasped her to him and kissed her. Disgusted, she 'tore herself free' from his grip (Freud, 1905a, p. 28). She nevertheless continued to meet him. Nor, she said, did she ever mention the office episode to anyone until she told Freud about it.

Freud in turn outrageously claimed that Dora's disgust at Herr K pressing a kiss on her in this episode was 'entirely and completely hysterical'. After all, he said, 'I happen to know Herr K [...] and he was still quite young and of prepossessing appearance' (Freud, 1905a, pp. 28, 29n.3).

Adding insult to injury, Freud attributed Dora's disgust aged thirteen or fourteen on this occasion, to hysterical displacement of the genital sensation evoked in her by 'the pressure of [Herr K's] erect member against her body' onto the oral region of her mouth. Why? Because, said Freud, she had overindulged in 'sensual sucking' when she was a baby (Freud, 1905a, pp. 28, 30).

During her treatment by Freud when she was eighteen, Dora told him about her father's sexual affair with Frau K. She also conveyed her embittered feeling that 'she had been handed over to Herr K' in exchange for his tolerating this affair (Freud, 1905a, p. 34). It may well have also been the reason why her parents turned a blind eye to Herr K sending her flowers every day, when he was staying nearby, giving her valuable presents, and spending all his spare time in her company.

In the past she too had turned a blind eye, not to Herr K's attentions to her, but to her father's affair with Frau K. After Herr K sexually propositioned her by the lake when she was fifteen or sixteen, however, she repeatedly complained about her father's continuing affair with Frau K.

Freud connected one of her hysterical symptoms – a nervous cough – to this affair. He argued that it resulted from Dora identifying with Frau K in oral sex with her father. After all, Freud added, Dora too enjoyed oral gratification in the form of thumbsucking when she was a child.

> She remembered very well that in her childhood she had been a thumbsucker. Her father, too, recollected breaking her of the habit after it had persisted into her fourth or fifth year. Dora herself had a clear picture of a scene from her early childhood in which she was sitting on the floor in a corner sucking her left thumb and at the same time tugging with her right hand at the lobe of her brother's ear as he sat quietly beside her. (Freud, 1905a, p. 51)

Freud also speculated that Dora's preoccupation with her father's affair with Frau K was due to jealousy since she herself sexually desired Frau K. The two women were very close. They shared a bedroom when Dora stayed with the K family, and Frau K confided in Dora all the difficulties of her married life. Dora in turn praised Frau K's 'adorable white body' in terms more suited, said Freud, to a lover than to 'a defeated rival' (Freud, 1905a, p. 61). And it was Frau K telling Herr K about Dora's interest in reading books about sexual matters that Herr K used in seeking to discredit, as product of a sexually fevered imagination, Dora's account of his sexually propositioning her by the lake.

Having recounted all this at the start of his Dora case study, Freud devoted most of its remaining pages to detailing and psychoanalyzing two of her dreams. The first one occurred some weeks after her treatment began. In recalling it Dora said:

> A house was on fire. My father was standing beside my bed and woke me up. I dressed quickly. Mother wanted to stop and save her jewel-case; but Father said: 'I refuse to let myself and my two children be burnt for the sake of your jewel-case'. We hurried downstairs, and as soon as I was outside I woke up. (Freud, 1905a, p. 64)

Dora had this self-same dream on three consecutive nights after the occasion when, after sexually propositioning her by the lake, Herr K came into the room where she was sleeping.

Her associations to the 'jewel-case' in this dream included his having given her one. Together with other associations, this led Freud to interpret the dream to Dora as involving her telling herself,

> 'This man [Herr K] is persecuting me; he wants to force his way into my room. My "jewel-case" [female genital] is in danger, and if anything happens it will be Father's fault'. For that reason you chose a situation which expresses the opposite – a danger from which your father is *saving* you. (Freud, 1905a, p. 69, italics in original)

Evidently, Freud told Dora, she had summoned up her childhood love for her father in her dream to protect her against the fire of her sexual desire for Herr K. Why, though, did she have the same dream during her treatment with Freud? Because, he said, she wished her father would protect her from him.

A few weeks later she told Freud another dream, of which she said,

> I was walking about in a town which I did not know. I saw streets and squares which were strange to me. Then I came into a house where I lived, went to my room, and found a letter from Mother lying there. [...] I then saw a thick wood before me which I went into, and there I asked a man whom I met. He said to me: 'Two and a half hours more.' [...] Then I was at home. [...] I walked into the porter's lodge, and enquired for our flat. The maidservant opened the door to me [...] After she had answered I went to my room, but not the least sadly, and began reading a big book that lay on my writing-table. (Freud, 1905a, p. 94)

Free associating to the letter from her mother in the dream, and after being reminded of the suicide letter she had written, Dora again recalled the occasion when Herr K sexually propositioned her by the lake. What words had he used on this occasion? 'You know I get nothing from my wife', Dora replied (Freud, 1905a, p. 98).

Why, though, did the dream end with her 'reading a big book'? To this Dora recalled looking in an encyclopaedia for the symptoms of appendicitis. When had she thought she had these symptoms? Freud asked. 'Nine months' after the occasion when Herr K sexually propositioned her, she said (Freud, 1905a, p. 103).

Learning this, Freud pointed out that her love of Herr K had evidently not stopped with this occasion since nine months later she imagined giving birth to his child. Freud also wondered why Dora mentioned 'two and a half hours more' in recounting this dream – a time span she replaced with 'two hours' at the start of her next appointment (Freud, 1905a, p. 94, n.3).

This was followed by a further appointment at the end of December 1900. It was her last one, she told Freud. She had decided to end her treatment with him. When had she made this decision? he asked. Two weeks previously, she replied, the same amount of notice a maidservant or governess gives her employer, he observed.

This reminded Dora that a couple of days before Herr K sexually propositioned her, she learnt from his children's governess that he had made love to her saying 'he got nothing from his wife' (Freud, 1905a, p. 106). But then he ceased to care for this woman. After giving him time to change his mind, and after this did not happen, she quit her employment with him.

Infuriated, it seems, by Herr K using the same words as he had used with the governess when he sexually propositioned her, Dora nevertheless gave him time to repeat his proposal. When, after two weeks, he failed to do so, she told her parents about his having sexually propositioned her. Learning this from Dora, Freud observed:

> Your father's relations with Frau K. – and it was probably only for this reason that you lent them your support for so long – made it certain that her consent to a divorce could be obtained; and you can get anything you like out of your father. [...] So it must have been a bitter piece of disillusionment for you when the effect of your charges against Herr K. was not that he renewed his proposals but that he replied instead with denials and slanders. [...] I know now – and this is what you do not want to be reminded of – that you *did* fancy that Herr K.'s proposals were serious, and that he would not leave off until you had married him. (Freud, 1905a, p. 108, italics in original)

Why, though, did Dora quit her treatment with Freud just as it was beginning to reveal more of what was unconsciously causing her psychological ills? Because, Freud argued in a postscript to his account of her case, he did not address in time her transference onto him of her feelings about Herr K.

'What are transferences?' he asked more generally.

> They are new editions or facsimiles of the [unconscious] impulses and phantasies which are aroused and made conscious during the progress of the analysis [...] they replace some earlier person by the

> person of the physician. [...] Some of these transferences have a content which differs from that of their model in no respect whatever except for the substitution. [...] Others are more ingeniously constructed [...] by cleverly taking advantage of some real peculiarity in the physician's person or circumstances and attaching themselves to that. (Freud, 1905a, p. 116)

Freud ended this postscript with further details about Dora. Fifteen months after she quit her treatment with him at the end of 1900, he recalled, she took revenge on the Ks. Visiting them to condole with them about the death of one of their children, she told Frau K, 'I know you have an affair with my father'. On the same visit she obtained from Herr K 'an admission of the scene by the lake which he had disputed, and brought the news of her vindication home to her father' (Freud, 1905a, p. 121).

This does not reflect particularly well on Dora. Nor does a report from the psychoanalyst Felix Deutsch that he had been told by someone that she was 'one of the most repulsive hysterics' he had ever met (Deutsch, 1957, p. 43).

Some years later the historian of ideas Michel Foucault (1976) argued that there was nothing new or radical as Freud more or less explicitly claimed in his talking openly about sex with Dora and his other patients. After all, Foucault maintained, the practice of the Catholic confessional has for centuries involved inciting penitents to confess and talk about themselves in sexual terms, thereby producing them as essentially sexual beings. This perspective informs the account of Dora provided by Lisa Appignanesi and John Forrester in their book, *Freud's Women*. Rather different accounts can be found in the book *In Dora's Case*, edited by Charles Bernheimer and Claire Kahane; in the psychoanalyst Jonathan Lear's book, *Freud*; and in another psychoanalyst Jean-Michel Quinodoz's book, *Reading Freud*.

> *SUMMARY:* Freud used his published case study of Dora to illustrate the value of dreams in psychoanalytic treatment, and to highlight the importance of psychoanalysts attending to the patient's transference onto them of their experience of other significant people in their lives.

HANS'S PHOBIA

Freud's case study of Dora was published the same year, 1905, as his book *Three Essays on the Theory of Sexuality*. He based this book on his self-analysis and on his treatment of patients like Dora. To discover more direct evidence about sexuality, particularly its development in early childhood, Freud encouraged his friends and students to provide him with direct observations of 'the sexual life of children' (Freud, 1909a, p. 6).

This was the starting point of his second long case study. It began with his friend, a music critic, Max Graf, the husband of one of his patients, Olga Hönig, volunteering to observe and send Freud observations of his and Olga's son, Herbert, now known in the history of psychoanalysis as Hans.

Quoting from these observations, Freud noted that when Hans was three and a half years old, he was preoccupied with his penis. This included his touching it in front of his mother, whereupon she told him, 'If you do that, I shall send for Dr. A. to cut off your widdler. And then what'll you widdle with?' 'With my bottom', he nonchalantly replied. Nor was he upset when he soon after saw his seven-day-old sister, Hanna, having a bath. '[H]er widdler's still quite small', he said, reassuring himself. 'When she grows up it'll get bigger all right' (Freud, 1909a, pp. 7–8, 11).

Fifteen months later, by which time he was four and a quarter years old, Hans was not so nonchalant. His father reported that he had 'developed a nervous disorder' and was afraid a horse would bite him in the street. About the same time, in January 1908, Hans woke up in tears one morning. 'When I was asleep I thought you were gone and I had no Mummy to coax [cuddle] with', he told her (Freud, 1909a, pp. 22, 23).

A couple of days later he went to the park with his nursemaid. But in the street he began to cry and asked to be taken home, his anxiety making him want to cuddle with his mother. Why, though, his anxiety? The answer was revealed, at least in part, when after his mother successfully persuaded him the next day to go out with her, he became anxious in the street, saying he was frightened a horse would bite him.

What was the cause of this fear? After all, Hans's father told him, horses don't bite. 'But white horses bite', Hans replied. He had heard a friend's father tell her, he explained, when she was near a cart with a white horse, 'Don't put your finger to the white horse or it'll bite you' (Freud, 1909a, p. 29).

He had become phobic not only of horses. He had also become phobic of large animals at the zoo. At least he refused to see a giraffe or elephant there despite having previously been amused by them.

This was followed by his being frightened by a dream, of which he said,

> In the night there was a big giraffe in the room and a crumpled one; and the big one called out because I took the crumpled one away from it. Then it stopped calling out; and then I sat down on top of the crumpled one. [...] [T]he crumpled one was all lying on the floor [...] I held it in my hand for a bit, till the big one had stopped calling out [...] Because I had taken away the little one from it. (Freud, 1909a, pp. 37, 38)

With this dream, argued his father, Hans repeated his habit of getting into bed with him and his wife early in the morning despite his warning his wife not to allow this. 'Call out as much as you like! But Mummy [the crumpled giraffe] takes me into bed all the same, and Mummy belongs to me!' said Freud in interpreting this as Hans's message to his father (Freud, 1909a, pp. 39–40).

This interpretation was soon after confirmed for Freud by Hans imagining himself and his father crawling under the ropes enclosing sheep at the zoo, and smashing a window pane. It signified, said Freud, Hans's wish to do what his father did with his mother – something forbidden such as forcing his way into an enclosed space or smashing a pane of glass.

Hans's horse phobia nevertheless persisted. He was particularly bothered by what horses wear in front of their eyes and by the black around their mouths. Noting the similarity of this to Hans's father's black spectacles and black moustache, Freud told Hans that perhaps because he was so fond of his mother, he was frightened of his father. 'But why do you think I'm angry with you?' Hans's father interrupted, 'have I ever scolded you or hit you?' 'Oh yes! You have hit me', Hans replied, giving the example of his father hitting him after Hans headbutted him in the stomach that morning (Freud, 1909a, p. 42).

He was also frightened for his father, it transpired. This emerged after he admitted that he worried when horses dragged a heavy van that they might fall down. This had happened, he explained, to a horse pulling a bus. Indeed this was the starting point of his horse phobia. It began in January 1908 when he saw 'a big heavy horse fall down'. Perhaps, Freud speculated, it caused him to wish that his father would likewise 'fall down […] and be dead', this resulting in anxiety which he wanted to allay by cuddling with his mother (Freud, 1909a, pp. 51–52).

Subsequently Hans was more openly defiant against his father. Perhaps this was because he was no longer afraid for, or of him. Perhaps not. Certainly he was not reassured by a fantasy he now had in which, he said, 'I was in the bath, and then the plumber came and unscrewed it. Then he took a big borer and stuck it into my stomach'. His father interpreted this as Hans saying to himself, 'I was in bed with Mummy. Then Daddy came and drove me away. With his big penis he pushed me out of my place by Mummy' (Freud, 1909a, p. 65).

Hans, though, had other things on his mind. He was trying to figure out the reason for his mother's 'heavily loaded stomach' when he stayed with his parents in Gmunden (some distance from Vienna) prior to his sister Hanna's birth. He also wondered how Hanna got into his mother's stomach. His speculations included his playing with an India-rubber doll. Describing this play, Hans's father recalled,

> [Hans] had pushed a small penknife in through the opening [in the doll] [...] and had then torn the doll's legs apart so as to let the knife drop out. He had said to the nurse-maid, pointing between the doll's legs: 'Look, there's its widdler!' (Freud, 1909a, p. 84)

Saying more about this doll, Hans told his father,

> I tore its legs apart. Do you know why? Because there was a knife inside it belonging to Mummy. I put it in at the place where the button squeaks, and then I tore apart its legs and it came out there. (Freud, 1909a, p. 84)

Prompted by this, it seems, Hans's parents told him about children growing inside their mother's tummy. To this they added that the child is born by being pressed out of the mother's body like a 'lumf' ['pooh'] (Freud, 1909a, p. 87).

They did not, however, explain how the child is originally conceived. Instead Hans's father was much more interested in Freud's interpretation of Hans's horse phobia in terms of his having seen a horse fall down, this prompting the anxiety-making wish in Hans that his father would fall down and die.

This was followed by another conversation between father and son:

> Father: 'Did you often get into bed with Mummy at Gmunden?'
> Hans: 'Yes'.
> Father: 'And you used to think to yourself you were Daddy?'
> Hans: 'Yes'.

> Father: 'And then you felt afraid of Daddy?'
> Hans: 'You know everything; I didn't know anything'.
> Father: 'When [your friend] Fritzl fell down you thought: "If only Daddy would fall down like that!" And when the lamb butted you you thought: "If only it would butt Daddy!" "Can you remember the funeral at Gmunden?" [...]'
> Hans: 'Yes. What about it?'
> Father: 'You thought then that if only Daddy were to die you'd be Daddy'.
> Hans: 'Yes'.
>
> (Freud, 1909a, p. 90)

That evening Hans talked about children with whom he was friends. He imagined them in bed with him. Soon after, on being questioned by his father about these children, another conversation took place between them:

> Father: 'You know quite well a boy can't have any children'.
> Hans: 'I know. I was their Mummy before, now I'm their Daddy'.
> Father: 'And who's the children's Mummy?'
> Hans: 'Why, Mummy, and you're their Grandaddy'.
>
> (Freud, 1909a, pp. 96–97)

This seemingly involved a fantasy in which Hans, not his father, had children with his mother. A couple of days later he recounted a dream or fantasy in which a plumber came and took away his behind with a pair of pincers and gave him another, and then did the same with his penis, his widdler. Learning this, his father asked him whether the plumber replaced his behind and his widdler with a bigger behind and widdler, because he wanted to be like him? Yes, he did indeed want to be like him, Hans replied.

Reassured that one day this would indeed be the case, Hans was cured of his horse phobia not long before his fifth birthday in early May 1908, four months after this phobia had begun. Freud attributed its origin to Hans being 'a little Oedipus' who wanted to have his father 'out of the way' so he might have his mother to himself to sleep with as he did in Gmunden when his father was away (Freud, 1909a, p. 111).

It was here in Gmunden that he had overheard his friend's father, when he was about to go away, tell her not to put her finger near a white horse lest it bite. It was not, however, with this that Freud ended his case study of Hans. Rather he ended it by saying that psychoanalytic treatment aims to enable 'the patient to obtain a conscious grasp of his unconscious wishes' (Freud, 1909a, p. 120).

In Hans's case, contrast his horse phobia was, it seems, cured by his learning and acquiring confidence that one day he would become a father. He acquired this confidence, however by confessing his 'wish to be married to his mother and to have many children by her' and by making his father innocuous by imagining him not as his father but as his grandfather married to his grandmother (Freud, 1909a, p. 131).

Had he been Hans's psychoanalyst, Freud added, he would have enlightened him, as his parents failed to do, about sexual intercourse – 'copulation' – as the means by which babies are conceived (Freud, 1909a, p. 145). Today, thanks largely to Freud and psychoanalysis, children are much more readily enlightened about their origin and that of their siblings than was Hans.

Despite the failure of Hans's parents to enlighten him on this matter, Freud was grateful to Hans's father for his observations of Hans. Expressing his gratitude to Hans's father in lectures about psychoanalysis in Massachusetts in September 1909, Freud said of his resulting case study of Hans (in which he misremembered Hans's age at the time of his phobia as five, not four),

> I myself have recently been fortunate enough to obtain a fairly complete picture of the somatic [bodily] instinctual manifestations of a child's erotic life from the analysis of a five-year-old boy [...] carried out with a correct technique by his own father (Freud, 1910a, p. 43)

Credit for pioneering the psychoanalysis of children, however, does not usually go to Hans's father, Max Graf. Instead it goes to Hermine Hug-Hellumuth on the basis of the publication in 1915 of her book, *A Young Girl's Diary*, with a preface by Freud. Better known are other pioneering publications about child analysis. They include a paper, 'The development of a child', presented by Melanie Klein to the Hungarian Psychoanalytical Society in 1919 (and published in 1921), and a book by Freud's psychoanalyst daughter, Anna Freud, *Introduction to the Technique of Child Analysis*, first published in 1926.

> *SUMMARY:* Freud's account of Max Graf's observations and psychoanalysis of his four-year-old son Hans's horse phobia reveals its source in Hans displacing onto horses his wish that his father were dead so he could have his mother to himself. Hans's phobia was resolved by his becoming conscious of his otherwise anxiety-making wish to become a father and have children with his mother.

12

THE RAT MAN'S OBSESSION

↓
This would now be known as clinical OCD.

In early October 1907, Freud began treating a twenty-nine-year-old lawyer, Ernst Lanzer, whom he affectionately referred to as the Rat Man. Ever since his early childhood, Lanzer had been plagued with obsessions involving fear that something might happen to his father. His obsessions, akin to those now diagnosed as evidence of obsessive compulsive disorder (OCD), had become particularly intense over the four years preceding the start of his treatment by Freud.

Lanzer had tried various treatments for these obsessions. None had helped except hydrotherapy, and that only because he met an acquaintance at the sanatorium where he had this treatment, which resulted in his having 'regular sexual intercourse' (Freud, 1909b, p. 158). Otherwise, he only occasionally had sexual intercourse. Anyway, he was disgusted by prostitutes, felt his sex life was stunted, admitted that it had included masturbation when he was fifteen or sixteen, and that he did not have any experience of sexual intercourse until he was twenty-six.

Why, though, did he begin his treatment with Freud by telling him all this? Because he knew Freud was interested in psychosexual development? That was a factor. Certainly he knew that Freud had theories about sex. But the only book by Freud which he had even glanced at was *The Psychopathology of Everyday Life*, in which sex is scarcely mentioned.

Having established all this in their first meetings together, Freud told Lanzer that his psychoanalytic treatment method depended on patients saying whatever occurred to them, however unpleasant, unimportant, irrelevant, or meaningless it might seem. This prompted Lanzer to recall that whenever he was tormented by a criminal impulse, he went to see a friend who assured him that he was 'a man of irreproachable conduct'. He also remembered sexual experience from his early childhood when he imagined that if he had sexual thoughts his 'father might die' (Freud, 1909b, p. 162).

It was only after saying all this and more that he at last told Freud the obsession for which he was particularly keen to get treatment. It had begun when he was told by an army captain about a particularly horrible eastern punishment. So saying, Lanzer got off Freud's psychoanalytic couch and begged Freud to excuse him from saying any more.

But that was impossible, said Freud. His treatment method depended on patients saying whatever occurred to them. He nevertheless sought to help Lanzer continue with his account of this obsession. At this Lanzer said of the punishment with which he was obsessed: '[T]he criminal was tied up ... a pot was turned upside down on his buttocks ... some *rats* were put into it ... and they ... *bored their way in* ...'. 'Into his anus', suggested Freud. At this Lanzer's face showed '*horror at pleasure of his own of which he himself was unaware*' as he went on to say of this rat punishment that the idea occurred to him that it was happening to someone of whom he was very fond (Freud, 1909b, pp. 166–167, italics in original).

Prompted by Freud to say who this person was, Lanzer admitted it was a woman he particularly admired. After further prompting or pressure from Freud, he added that he also thought about the rat punishment being applied to his father – a nonsensical thought, noted Freud, since Lanzer's father had died many years before.

As for the rat punishment, soon after learning about it from the army captain, Lanzer was told by this selfsame captain that he owed an army lieutenant money as repayment for a minor post office bill which he had incurred and that the lieutenant had paid for him. No sooner did Lanzer learn this than he decided he must not pay the lieutenant the money he owed him since, if he did, the woman he admired and his father would be subjected to the rat punishment. This led him to various contorted ways of avoiding paying this debt – a debt which he had in fact already paid.

Another related obsession involved Lanzer removing a stone from the road lest it cause an accident to the carriage in which the woman he admired was due to travel. After removing this stone, he put it back on the road because, explained Freud, a 'battle' raged within Lanzer between conscious love and unconscious hatred of this woman (Freud, 1909b, p. 191).

A similar battle, it seemed, caused what Freud described as Lanzer's 'father complex'. Examples included Lanzer thinking, on first having sexual intercourse when he was twenty-six, 'This is glorious! One might murder one's father for this!' (Freud, 1909b, pp. 200, 201). Freud put this together with the fact that, shortly after his father's death, Lanzer, then aged twenty, felt impelled to indulge in 'masturbatory activities'. On this basis Freud speculated that Lanzer had been 'guilty of some sexual misdemeanour' when he was a young child for which his father punished him (Freud, 1909b, pp. 203, 205).

This prompted Lanzer to recall that his mother had repeatedly described the following incident, of which he had no memory. It had occurred when he was three or four years old.

> [H]e had done something naughty ['he had *bitten* some one'], for which his father had given him a beating. [At this Lanzer] had flown into a terrible rage and had hurled abuse at his father even while he was under his blows. But as he knew no bad language, he had called him all the names of common objects that he could think of, and had screamed: 'You lamp! You towel! You plate!' and so on. His father, shaken by such an outburst of elemental fury, had stopped beating him, and had declared: 'The child will be either a great man or a great criminal!' The patient [Lanzer] believed that the scene made a permanent impression upon himself as well as upon his father. His father, he said, never beat him again; and he also attributed to this experience a part of the change which came over his own character. From that time forward he was a coward – out of fear of the violence of his own rage. His whole life long, moreover, he was terribly afraid

> of blows, and used to creep away and hide, filled with terror and indignation, when one of his brothers or sisters was beaten. (Freud, 1909b, pp. 205–206)

He could not bear to stay anywhere near them then lest their being beaten provoke ungovernable seeming hatred and fury against his father, which he apparently kept repressed and unconscious.

He only became conscious of this hatred through his transference experience of it in relation to Freud, against whom he hurled verbal abuse just as, according to his mother, he had hurled verbal abuse at his father when he was three or four years old. In hurling abuse at Freud he despaired. He got off the psychoanalytic couch and roamed around Freud's consulting room. Why? Because, he realized, he thereby avoided being near Freud, whom he feared might beat him as his father had beaten him when, as a young child, he had hurled verbal abuse at him.

Lanzer's recovery of his previously repressed and unconscious early childhood hatred of his father by transferring it onto his experience of Freud marked a 'turning-point' in his treatment (Freud, 1909b, p. 209). It led him to recall further material, on the basis of which Freud arrived at the following understanding and interpretation of his rat punishment obsession:

> What the rat punishment stirred up more than anything else was his *anal erotism*, which had played an important part in his childhood and had been kept in activity for many years by a constant irritation due to worms. In this way rats came to have the meaning of '*money*'. The patient gave an indication of this connection by reacting to the word '*Ratten*' [German for 'rats'] with the association '*Raten*' [German for 'instalments']. (Freud, 1909b, pp. 213–214, italics in original)

Hence Lanzer's obsession with paying or not paying the money which the army captain said he owed the lieutenant.

On the basis of this and other details gleaned from Lanzer's psychoanalytic treatment, Freud arrived at the following interpretation of his crippling rat punishment obsession:

> [When] the captain had told [Lanzer] about the rat punishment [...] a connection [was] set up with the scene from his childhood in which he himself had bitten some one. The captain – a man who could defend such punishments – had become a substitute for [Lanzer's] father, and had thus drawn down upon himself a part of the reviving animosity which had burst out, on the original occasion, against his cruel father. The idea which came into his consciousness for a moment, to the effect that something of the sort might happen to some one he was fond of, is probably to be translated into a wish such as 'You ought to have the same thing done to you!' aimed at the [captain] teller of the [rat punishment] story, but through him at his father. (Freud, 1909b, p. 217)

It was repression of hatred of his father and its conflict with his conscious love of him, together with similar conflict between unconscious hatred and conscious love of the woman he admired, that caused Lanzer's obsession with causing or not causing them to become victims of the rat punishment. Through thus interpreting Lanzer's symptoms, Freud helped him recover from this crippling obsession less than a year after his psychoanalytic treatment began.

Meanwhile, thanks seemingly to what he learned during his treatment of Lanzer, Freud developed an account of what has come to be known as the anal character. Freud described it as marked by 'orderly, parsimonious and obstinate' behaviour. It originates developmentally, he argued, in early childhood resistance to potty training, pleasure in holding back faeces, and in doing 'unseemly things' with them. The three anal character traits of orderliness, parsimoniousness, and obstinacy result, he maintained, from 'sublimation' of their developmental origin in the 'anal erotism' of early childhood (Freud, 1908c, pp. 169, 170, 171).

This account by Freud of the anal character still has currency today. So does his account of Lanzer's anal rat punishment obsession. But his understanding of Lanzer's case has also been criticized. The psychoanalyst Jean-Michel Quinodoz (2005), for instance, has criticized Freud for neglecting his role as a motherly figure in Lanzer's life. The psychoanalyst Claire Cripwell (2011) has also drawn attention to maternal factors in this case. She speculates that Lanzer's repressed hatred of his father such that it was unconscious might have been due to his mother being so preoccupied with his sister dying when he was three or four years old, she could not contain and thereby enable him to experience his anger and hatred of his father at that age as something he could contain and know about rather than repress.

> *SUMMARY:* Freud interpreted the crippling rat obsession of his patient, Ernst Lanzer, as due to conflict between repressed and unconscious hatred of, and rage against his father and conscious love of him. Freud's psychoanalytic treatment of Lanzer also led him to formulate his theory of what is now known, thanks to him, as a developmentally determined anal character type. It has also led to subsequent psychoanalytic attention to maternal factors in this case.

SCHREBER'S SCHIZOPHRENIA

Unlike his case studies of Dora, Hans, and his Rat Man patient, Ernst Lanzer, Freud based his fourth long case study on the published account by a patient, Daniel Paul Schreber, of his mental illness. In doing so Freud variously described Schreber's illness as dementia praecox, psychosis, or schizophrenia, now defined by the American Psychiatric Association as including delusions, hallucinations, and disorganized speech.

Schreber's early history included his birth in Leipzig in Germany on 25 July 1842, and his becoming a judge like his older brother, Gustav, who committed suicide when he was thirty-eight, after which Schreber married the following year, 1878, and became unhappy that the marriage remained childless. He was also seemingly very unhappy after being defeated as a candidate in parliamentary elections in 1884.

Later that year he became so mentally disturbed he was hospitalized many miles from his home town, Leipzig, in Sonnenstein. Two months later, however, in early December 1884, he was returned to a psychiatric clinic in Leipzig. There he was treated by a psychiatrist, Paul Flechsig, for whose help he was so grateful he rewarded him with money around the time of his recovery and discharge home in June 1885.

After that, all seemingly went well with Schreber until June 1893 when he learnt of his appointment as president of the district court in Dresden. He now several times dreamt that he was again mentally ill. He also woke one morning with the thought that it would 'be very nice to be a woman submitting to the act of copulation' (Freud, 1911b, p. 13).

After taking up his new appointment early that October he soon became so unwell that, on 21 November, he was readmitted to the psychiatric clinic in Leipzig where he was again treated by Flechsig. He was then transferred in June 1894 to a nearby asylum in Lindenhof from where, a couple of weeks later, he was again hospitalized in Sonnenstein. It was here he wrote the memoir of his mental illness which was published. This occurred soon after his discharge in December 1902.

In this memoir, according to Freud, Schreber described 'visual and auditory illusions' dominating 'the whole of his feeling and thought'. He also recorded his belief that 'he was dead and decomposing, that he was suffering from the plague' and that 'his body was being handled in all kinds of revolting ways'. Preoccupation with this resulted in his becoming 'inaccessible to any other impression' and to his sitting 'perfectly rigid and motionless for hours' (Freud, 1911b, pp. 13, 14).

Apart from these obvious 'psychomotor symptoms', noted the asylum's director in 1899, Schreber showed no 'signs of confusion'. Indeed, the director added,

> [Schreber's] mind is collected, his memory is excellent, he has at his disposal a very considerable store of knowledge [...] takes an interest in following events in the world of politics, science and art, etc., and is constantly occupied with such matters [...] Since for the last nine months Herr Präsident Schreber has taken his meals daily at my family board [...] Whatever the subject was that came up for discussion (apart, of course, from his delusional ideas), whether it concerned events in the field of administration and law, of politics, art, literature or social life – in short, whatever the topic, Dr. Schreber gave evidence of a lively interest, a well-informed mind, a good memory, and a sound judgement; his ethical outlook, moreover, was one which it was impossible not to endorse. (Freud, 1911b, p. 15)

It was evidence that non-schizophrenic or non-psychotic states of mind coexisted in Schreber alongside schizophrenic, psychotic, or delusional states of mind – an aspect of psychosis highlighted years later by the psychoanalyst Wilfred Bion (1957).

Schreber's delusional experiences included the belief that, during his March or April 1894 treatment by Flechsig in Leipzig, 'a conspiracy' against him 'was brought to a head'. Of this conspiracy, Schreber said,

> Its object was to contrive that, when once my nervous complaint had been recognized as incurable or assumed to be so, I should be handed over to a certain person in a particular manner: my soul was to be delivered up to him, but my body – owing to a misapprehension of what I have described [...] as the purpose underlying the Order of Things – was to be transformed into a female body, and as such surrendered to the person in question [Flechsig] with a view to sexual abuse. (in Freud, 1911b, p. 19)

Schreber subsequently became convinced that 'God Himself had played the part of accomplice, if not of instigator; in the plot whereby [his] soul was to be murdered and [his] body used like a strumpet'. He also recalled becoming aware the following November 1895 that he had been 'transformed into a woman' – an idea that became 'clearly conscious' in him while writing his memoir (in Freud, 1911b, p. 19).

What was the cause of this and Schreber's other delusions? Why, for instance, did he believe that Flechsig had tried to, or had succeeded in making him a victim of 'soul-murder' by penetrating him with 'forty to sixty sub-divisions of the Flechsig soul' (Freud, 1911b, pp. 35, 39–40)?

Perhaps, given his gratitude to Flechsig when he was first treated by him from October 1884 until June 1885, Schreber felt sexually attracted to him. As evidence in support of this speculation, Freud cited the fact that when his wife was briefly away from home prior to his 'nervous collapse' in November 1893, Schreber experienced 'a quite extraordinary number' of wet dreams 'all in one night' (Freud, 1911b, p. 45).

Perhaps his wife's presence protected him from unwanted homosexual feelings for men and from 'homosexual phantasies' accompanying these wet dreams, Freud speculated. To this he added the possibility that Schreber's sexual desire for Flechsig was based on his transferring onto Flechsig 'a longing, intensified to an erotic pitch, for his father and brother' (Freud, 1911b, pp. 45, 50).

Why, though, if Schreber sexually desired Flechsig, did he develop the paranoid belief that Flechsig persecuted him? And why did Schreber replace this belief with the belief that 'God' evoked 'voluptuous sensations' in him (Freud, 1911b, p. 48)?

By way of answer, Freud argued that, for Schreber, God constituted a deity modelled on his 'eminent physician' father, Moritz Schreber, renowned for his 1856 book, *Medical Indoor Gymnastics* (Freud, 1911b, p. 52). Following Moritz's death in 1861, Freud suggested, Schreber derived his idea of God from adulation of his older brother, Gustav, in whose footsteps he had followed in becoming a judge like him.

Perhaps, Freud speculated, it was Schreber's lack of a son – 'who might have consoled him for the loss of his father and brother' and thereby 'drained off his unsatisfied homosexual affections' – which caused Schreber to think

> [I]f he were a woman he would manage the business of having children more successfully [...] If that were so, then his delusion that as a result of his emasculation the world was to be peopled with 'a new race of men, born from the spirit of Schreber' [...] would also be designed to offer him an escape from his childlessness. (Freud, 1911b, p. 58)

It was not, however, in terms of Schreber's childlessness that Freud psychoanalyzed Schreber's ills. Instead Freud psychoanalyzed them, particularly Schreber's paranoia, in terms of the view – which Freud at that time shared with his psychoanalytic colleagues Carl Jung and Sandor Ferenczi – that paranoia is due to homosexuality.

He also believed that homosexuality is rooted in a narcissistic stage in the child's psychosexual development. In this stage, he said,

> [The child] unifies his sexual instincts (which have hitherto been engaged in auto-erotic activities) in order to obtain a love-object; and he begins by taking himself, his own body, as his love-object, and only subsequently proceeds from this to the choice of some person other than himself as his object. [...] [I]t appears that many people linger unusually long in this condition, and that many of its features are carried over by them into the later stages of their development. What is of chief importance in the subject's self thus chosen as a love-object may already be the genitals. The line of development then leads on to the choice of an external object with similar genitals [...] People who are manifest homosexuals in later life have, it may be presumed, never emancipated themselves from the binding condition that the object of their choice must possess genitals like their own. (Freud, 1911b, pp. 60–61)

Having arrived at this theory of the roots of homosexuality in a narcissistic stage of psychosexual development, Freud proceeded to use this theory as the basis for his understanding of Schreber's paranoia about Flechsig.

It was due, he argued, to Schreber defending against homosexual desire for Flechsig with repression, reversal, and projection. He repressed the thought '*I* (a man) *love him* (a man)'. He then reversed this into the opposite thought 'I do not *love* him – I *hate* him'. Projecting his resulting hatred onto Flechsig, he developed the paranoid thought '*He* hates (persecutes) *me*' (Freud, 1911b, p. 63, italics in the original).

Having thus attributed Schreber's paranoia about Flechsig in terms of the defence mechanisms of repression, reversal, and paranoia, Freud focused on another aspect of Schreber's schizophrenia – his 'terrifying' delusion that the world was ending of which Freud reported

> Voices told him that the work of the past 14,000 years had now come to nothing, and that the earth's allotted span was only 212 years more [...] He himself was 'the only real man left alive', and the few human shapes that he still saw – the doctor, the attendants, the other patients – he explained as being 'miracled up, cursorily improvised men'. (Freud, 1911b, p. 68)

Why this delusion?

Because, Freud explained, Schreber had projected onto the external world the catastrophic emptiness that had occurred in his inner world. This emptiness was due to his having withdrawn from all attachment to anyone and anything outside himself. It was countered with another delusion: namely, that through being turned into a woman, he was being impregnated by God so as to be able to repopulate the world with 'a new race of men'. It was, insisted Freud, *'an attempt at recovery, a process of reconstruction'* (Freud, 1911b, pp. 20–21, 71, italics in original). This aspect of schizophrenia is helpfully further explained by the psychoanalyst Darian Leader in his book *What Is Madness?*

Long before that, Freud (1924) described delusions in psychosis as applying a patch to cover a gap in reality. Either way, he regarded psychosis as not amenable to psychoanalytic treatment. In psychotic states of mind, he argued, patients are so narcissistically wrapped up in themselves that they cannot form the transference relation to the psychoanalyst necessary for psychoanalytic treatment to proceed. This despite the fact that he argued that Schreber transferred experience of his father and brother onto his doctor, Flechsig (see p. 79 above).

Other psychoanalysts, notably Melanie Klein, have been more optimistic about treating psychosis psychoanalytically. Freud regarded Schreber's psychosis as rooted in a 'father-complex' (Freud, 1911b, p. 55). By contrast, Klein conceptualized psychosis in maternal terms. She attributed it to regression to a paranoid-schizoid stage in early infant psychological development. In this stage, she maintained, the infant defensively splits apart its experience of its mother, or at least parts of her body, such that it experiences her, on the one hand, as a good and loved breast and, on the other hand, as a bad and hated breast. Defending against overwhelming bad and hateful feelings within itself, the infant, according to Klein, projects these 'bad self' feelings onto its mother, in whom it identifies these feelings (Klein, 1946, p. 8).

The psychoanalyst Ronnie Laing and the psychiatrist Aaron Esterson (1964) reacted against this psychoanalytic account of psychosis or schizophrenia. They drew attention to the mother and other family relationship issues as cause of schizophrenic states of mind.

Laing's sometime psychiatrist colleague Morton Schatzman (1973) in turn highlighted paternal factors which might have caused Schreber's schizophrenia. He noted particularly the cruel child-rearing methods advocated by Schreber's father, Moritz, in his above-mentioned book, *Medical Indoor Gymnastics*, methods which included confining the child's body in a contraption designed to ensure their correct posture at the dining table.

Since the wholescale closure of mental hospitals, and their replacement in Britain by care in the community and by treatment of schizophrenia or psychosis with 'atypical' antipsychotic medication, psychoanalytic understanding of these conditions has been informed by the work of the above-mentioned psychoanalyst Wilfred Bion.

Years before this closure began, Bion (e.g.1962a, 1962b) drew on Freud's and Klein's understanding of Schreber's schizophrenia as involving projection of what he could not bear in himself – his hatred, for instance -- onto his doctor, Flechsig. Unlike Freud and Klein, Bion argued that such projection is a form of communication to which the psychoanalyst might helpfully respond by containing and transforming the sense-data experience projected onto them by the patient. Through the psychoanalyst's resulting response, the patient may thereby be enabled to contain this previously defended against, and projected experience in knowable and thinkable form.

This approach has been developed by psychoanalysts working with patients who are also being treated with the above-mentioned 'atypical' anti-psychotic medication. Recent examples can be found in articles by Lombardi (2005), Lombardi and Pola (2010), and Poyet (2019).

Others have sought to use the psychoanalytic understanding of schizophrenia or psychosis developed by Freud, Klein, Bion, and others to help those working with patients with this condition better understand what is going on in their mind. Just as Freud (see p. 78 above) and Bion (1957) observed that psychotic and non-psychotic states of mind can coexist, so does the psychoanalyst Brian Martindale and his colleague Alison Summers (2013). They illustrate this with the example of a woman patient whose psychosis included the paranoid delusion that people were breaking into her home through cracks in the floorboard. She nevertheless had sufficient presence of mind to seek help not from the police but from a doctor.

Martindale uses such examples to help nurses, families, and others involved with people diagnosed as psychotic or schizophrenic to better understand them. This includes using various examples, one of which involved a psychiatric nurse of whom Martindale says,

> [She] was trying to engage a man with a serious psychosis of many years duration and was trying to offer him 'simple' practical advice such as managing his debts, matters related to his housing and supporting him in taking medication. However this was not getting anywhere. It transpired she was not used to trying to make sense of the content of her patients' delusions and hallucinations. Once she was helped to tune into these she realized his hallucinatory voices (the content of which he had been wary of revealing to her) were telling him to not trust any advice. She was helped to take more seriously his life story and realized that after his mother had broken down (and had never fully recovered) when he was 11, he had resolved to be self-sufficient; he believed that needing help would be getting on to a 'slippery slope' from which there would be no recovery (just like his mother). [The nurse] then realized the naivety of her 'simply' trying to prove that she could be helpful, trustworthy and well intentioned, and that medication would necessarily help his hallucinations and 'paranoia'. She could now see that being in need of her help was subjectively a very great danger to him. Therefore a dialogue about whether any suggestion of hers was him getting onto the 'slippery slope' became a feature of her ongoing contact with him and he started to feel taken seriously. (Martindale, 2015, n.p.)

These and other examples are testimony to ways in which, although he seldom if ever knowingly treated patients with schizophrenia or psychosis, Freud paved the way – with his psychoanalytic understanding of Schreber's published account of his mental illness – for others to better understand the state of mind involved today.

SUMMARY: Freud understood Schreber's schizophrenia or psychosis as involving defences of repression, reversal, and projection rooted in a childhood 'father-complex'. Developments of this understanding have informed subsequent psychoanalytic accounts of this condition. They are used to help those involved with patients with schizophrenia or psychosis to better understand what might be going on in their mind.

THE WOLF MAN'S NIGHTMARE

In February 1910, a few months before completing his understanding of Schreber's schizophrenia, Freud began treating a wealthy Russian, Sergei Pankejeff. Although Sergei's problems were related to a gonorrhoeal infection which he had contracted five years before, when he was seventeen, it was on a nightmare Sergei suffered as a young child that Freud particularly focused in his resulting case study.

During the months preceding this nightmare, Sergei's parents had gone away, leaving him with his sister, who was two years older than him; with his Nanya or nursemaid who had begun looking after him after the death of her son; and with an English governess whose conflict with Sergei's Nanya was blamed for his bad behaviour after his parents returned home later that year.

Previously Sergei had been 'a very good-natured, tractable, and even quiet child'. Now he was 'discontented, irritable and violent, took offence on every possible occasion, and then flew into a rage and screamed like a savage' (Freud, 1918b, p.15). His grandmother attributed this alteration in his character to disagreements between his Nanya and governess. But, although the governess was dismissed, his behaviour did not improve.

Previously, when he was about three-and-a-quarter years old, his sister had 'seduced' him.

> [She took] hold of his penis and played with it, at the same time telling him incomprehensible stories about his Nanya, as though by way of explanation. His Nanya, she said, used to do the same thing with all kinds of people – for instance, with the gardener: she used to stand him on his head, and then take hold of his genitals. (Freud, 1918b, p. 20)

Not surprisingly, perhaps, Sergei did not like his sister. He avoided her. Nevertheless, having learnt from her about his Nanya's sexual activity with the gardener, he played with his penis in front of her, for which she reprimanded him by saying that 'children who did that […] got a "wound" in [that] place' (Freud, 1918b, p. 24).

Initially, Sergei was not apparently worried by this. Nor was he alarmed by seeing his sister's and her friend's lack of a penis when they urinated. Instead of acknowledging this lack, he told himself they urinated with their 'front bottom'. He was nevertheless upset, Freud contended, by images of castration evoked by his governess having described sugar-sticks as 'pieces of chopped-up snakes'; by remembering his father beating a snake with a stick; and by a story about a wolf using its tail as fishing bait whereupon it got broken off in frozen ice (Freud, 1918b, p. 25).

This upset contributed, it seems, to Sergei giving up playing with his penis and to his regression, according to Freud, to the 'sadistic-anal' stage of his psychosexual development. Examples for Freud of Sergei's sadism included tormenting his Nanya, catching flies and pulling off their wings, crushing beetles, imagining beating large animals, and indulging in fantasies about 'boys being chastised and beaten […] especially […] on the penis' (Freud, 1918b, p. 26).

Three-year-old Sergei also used 'fits of rage and scenes of fury', said Freud, to elicit 'punishments and beatings' from his father. This included an occasion when he redoubled 'his screams as soon as his father came towards him' (Freud, 1918b, pp. 27, 28). Another time he was particularly naughty and enraged when, despite Christmas coinciding with his birthday, he did not receive a double quantity of presents that Christmas Eve.

It was then, the night before his fourth birthday, that Sergei had his above-mentioned nightmare of which he said,

> I dreamt that it was night and that I was lying in my bed. (My bed stood with its foot towards the window; in front of the window there was a row of old walnut trees. I know it was winter when I had the dream, and night-time.) Suddenly the window opened of its own accord, and I was terrified to see that some white wolves were sitting on the big walnut tree in front of the window. There were six or seven of them. The wolves were quite white, and looked more like foxes or sheep-dogs, for they had big tails like foxes and they had their ears pricked like dogs when they pay attention to something. In great terror, evidently of being eaten up by the wolves, I screamed and woke up. [...] The only piece of action in the dream was the opening of the window; for the wolves sat quite still and without making any movement on the branches of the tree, to the right and left of the trunk, and looked at me. It seemed as though they had riveted their whole attention upon me. (Freud, 1918b, p. 29)

Freud speculated, on the basis of Sergei's free associations to this nightmare, that it revived and gave new traumatic meaning to a memory of himself witnessing the primal scene of his parents making love. Reconstructing this episode from what Sergei told him regarding his memory of it, Freud reported,

> [Sergei] was suffering at the time from malaria, an attack of which used to come on every day at a particular hour. [...] Probably for the very reason of this illness, he was in his parents' bedroom. [...] He had been sleeping in his cot, then, in his parents' bedroom, and woke up, perhaps because of his rising fever, in the afternoon [...] When he woke up, he witnessed a coitus *a tergo* [from behind], three times repeated; he was able to see his mother's genitals as well as his father's organ; and he understood the process as well as its significance. (Freud, 1918b, pp. 36–37)

Perhaps, Freud noted, this memory of having witnessed the primal scene of his parents' sexual intercourse might have resulted from Sergei having seen animals copulate such that he could see that, unlike the male, the female has no penis.

Either way, Freud argued, it gave new meaning to Sergei's previous 'inverted Oedipus complex' desire to take his mother's place in sexual intercourse with his father expressed in Sergei's naughtiness geared to secure punishment from him (Freud, 1918b, p. 119). It signified that realization of this father-oriented desire entailed his being without his penis like his mother.

It was Sergei's resulting castration anxiety or complex which, claimed Freud, contributed to his becoming anxious and terrified of a picture illustrating the story 'Little Red Riding Hood', with which his sister tormented him – a picture, perhaps reminiscent of an image of their father in the primal scene, since it showed a wolf 'standing upright, striding out with one foot, with its claws stretched out and its ears pricked' (Freud, 1918b, p. 30; see also Laplanche & Pontalis, 1968).

Sergei also remembered in connection with his nightmare a story told him by his grandfather. In it a tailor retaliates against a wolf jumping through the window of his workroom by pulling off the wolf's tail. Subsequently, seeing wolves approaching him in a forest, the tailor tries to escape by climbing a tree. But the wolves come after him. With them is the wolf whose tail the tailor had pulled off for which the wolf wanted revenge.

Following his nightmare Sergei was no longer full of rage and fury. He became passive and anxious. When he was four and a half years old, his mother sought to quell his anxiety by telling him Bible stories. This contributed to his warding off anxiety-making dreams by obsessively and compulsively kissing all the icons in his room, reciting prayers, and making 'innumerable signs of the cross upon himself and upon his bed' before going to sleep. These obsessional rituals continued until Sergei was ten years old when his then 'father-surrogate' tutor made it clear that he did not believe in religion (Freud, 1918b, pp. 61, 68).

It was due to other neurotic symptoms, beginning when he was seventeen, that, as indicated at the start of this chapter, Freud began treating Sergei in February 1910, treatment which was more or less successful when it ended in July 1914. Some years later, Sergei had more treatment with Freud. He was then treated by a psychiatrist, Ruth Mack Brunswick. Further details of his story can be found in the 1972 book *The Wolf Man*, edited by Muriel Gardiner. Freud's biographer, Peter Gay, in turn reported that, following the 1917–1918 Russian revolution, Sergei became sufficiently psychologically well and independent 'to marry, to face the loss of his family fortune, with a certain mature resignation, and to hold a job' (Gay, 1988, p. 292).

> SUMMARY: With his case history of his Wolf Man patient, Sergei Pankejeff, and especially with his analysis of Sergei's nightmare, occurring on the eve of his fourth birthday, Freud highlighted the bringing to an end of Sergei's inverted Oedipus complex desire for his father by castration complex fear of having no penis like his mother. This complex was followed by obsessional symptoms which ended due to the influence of a German tutor on Sergei when he was ten.

CONCLUSIONS TO PART III

With his five long case studies Freud laid the groundwork for the continuing development of psychoanalysis in terms of individual case studies today. Developing psychoanalysis on this basis and on the basis of Freud's self-analysis has often been criticized. Yet it is only through extrapolating from individual examples that we can arrive at universal truths, argued the historian of psychoanalysis John Forrester in his book *Thinking in Cases*.

What, then, can be learnt from Freud's five long case studies? His case study of Dora not only indicates the usefulness of dreams in psychoanalytic treatment. It also indicates the importance of psychoanalysts paying attention to ways in which their patients transfer onto them more or less unconscious feelings about other significant people in their lives.

With his second long case study Freud showed how Oedipal fear of, and for the father can be displaced onto a phobia. In this case Freud showed how four-year-old Hans displaced these feelings about his father onto a phobia of horses lest they bite him or fall down.

Freud's third long case study of his Rat Man patient, Ernst Lanzer, highlights the role of repressed and unconscious hatred in conflict with conscious love in obsessive compulsive disorder. It also contributed to Freud formulating his account of what, thanks to him, is now known as an anal character type.

Drawing for his fourth long case study on Schreber's published account of his schizophrenia, Freud showed how this condition – in this instance symptoms of paranoia and delusion – can be understood psychoanalytically. And, with his fifth and last long case study, of Sergei Pankejeff, Freud helped develop his theory linking the Oedipus and castration complex.

PART IV
CONSOLIDATING PSYCHOANALYSIS

In 1913, Freud's previous close friendship with the psychoanalyst Carl Gustav Jung ends due largely to Jung's rejection of the centrality Freud accorded to sex in psychoanalysis. While Jung founds analytical psychology, Freud consolidates his psychoanalytic theory of sex and repression, his account of what are now known as Freudian symbols, and his understanding of the Oedipal and intersubjective aspects of psychosexual development, subsequently modified in terms of attachment theory and in terms of a revised version of Freud's early seduction theory. Meanwhile, in lectures in 1915–1917, Freud consolidates his developmental psychology account of psychological symptom formation. He also consolidates his approach to psychoanalytic treatment which, as explained with clinical examples, continues in long- or short-term form today.

Introducing
carl Jung.

FREUD VERSUS JUNG

Jung was nearly twenty years younger than Freud. The son of a pastor, Jung was born on 26 July 1875 in Switzerland, where he studied medicine. After passing his final medical exams in Basel, he got psychiatric work, beginning in December 1900, at the Burghölzli mental hospital in Zurich. It was here, it seems, that he first learnt about psychoanalysis through being asked by the hospital's director, Eugen Bleuler (famous among other things for coining the term 'schizophrenia'), to present a summary of Freud's 1901 book, *On Dreams*.

Not long after, Jung sent Freud copies of his books *Studies in Word Association* and *The Psychogenesis of Mental Disease*. The first book was based on word association tests used by Jung and his colleagues at the Burghölzli to identify repressed or fragmented eruptions of feeling-toned complexes in patients with hysteria or schizophrenia. In the second book Jung used Freud's psychoanalytic ideas as means of understanding conditions now described as psychosis or schizophrenia.

When Jung first met Freud in Vienna in early March 1907, they talked long into the night. They met again at the first International Congress of Psychiatry and Neurology in Amsterdam that September. The following April 1908 they again met, this time in Salzburg, at that month's first congress of the International Psychoanalytic Association (IPA). At this congress Freud presented his case study of Ernst Lanzer (see Chapter 12 above), and Jung spoke about schizophrenia (then known as *dementia praecox*). Thanks largely, it seems, to Freud's high opinion of him, Jung was elevated to the role of editor of the IPA yearbook when it was established at this congress.

That autumn, 1908, Freud stayed with Jung at the Burghölzli. Here he hoped to persuade Jung 'to continue and complete [his] work by applying to psychoses what [he had] begun with neuroses' (Freud, 1908e, p. 168), something which Freud himself did with his case study of Schreber's schizophrenia (as described in Chapter 13 above).

The next year, 1909, Freud and Jung psychoanalyzed each other's dreams on their journey to and from Clark University in Massachusetts where, together with the psychoanalyst Sandor Ferenczi, they gave lectures about psychoanalysis that autumn. The same year saw the publication of Freud's above-mentioned Lanzer case in which he adopted Jung's 'complex' terminology in writing about Lanzer's 'father complex' (Freud, 1909b, p. 200). Freud again used this terminology in coining, for the first time, the term 'Oedipus complex' in an account of the sexual fantasies of pre-pubescent boys (Freud, 1910d, p. 171).

Freud's interest at that time in the Oedipus myth or story reflected his then shared interest with Jung in mythology. Like Jung, he also became interested in symbolism, about which he introduced many examples in the 1909 and 1911 editions of his book *The Interpretation of Dreams*.

He was not, however, sympathetic to Jung replacing his account of the conscious and unconscious mind with an account of two forms of thinking, verbal and symbolic. Freud (1911a) countered this by reiterating his psychoanalytic theory regarding unconscious and conscious, primary and secondary process thinking, ruled respectively by what he described as the pleasure and reality principle. Jung nevertheless went ahead with his replacement theory about verbal and symbolic thinking in his 1912 book, *Symbols of Transformation*.

Freud was particularly appalled by Jung saying of lectures he gave that autumn in New York,

> Naturally I also made room for those of my views which deviate in places from the hitherto existing conceptions, particularly in regard to the libido theory. I found that my version of psychoanalysis won over many people who until now had been put off by the problem of sexuality in neurosis. (Jung, 1912b, p. 515)

After further disagreements Freud suggested to Jung in January 1913 that they end their friendship, a suggestion with which Jung agreed.

That August, in lectures in London, Jung differentiated his psychological approach from that of Freud. He called his approach analytical psychology and replaced the centrality accorded to sex by Freud in psychoanalysis with a version of the libido which he described as 'vital energy […] *élan vital*' (Jung, 1913a, p. 248, italics in original).

At the next month's IPA congress, in Munich, Jung presented a paper about extrovert and introvert, outward-looking and inward-looking personality types. In doing so he rejected Freud's sexually based or 'materially-minded' attitude in favour of a more 'spiritually-minded' approach (Jung, 1913b, pp. 457–458).

This annoyed Freud. So did Jung's chairing of this IPA congress. He described it as 'disagreeable and incorrect' (Freud, 1914a, p. 45). Jung was nevertheless re-elected president of the IPA, a position from which he resigned the following April.

Meanwhile the 1914 IPA yearbook contained two articles by Freud criticizing Jung. In one article he objected to Jung's abandonment and betrayal of psychoanalysis by saying of Jung's approach,

> For sexual libido an abstract concept has been substituted, of which one may safely say that it remains mystifying and incomprehensible to wise men and fools alike. The Oedipus complex has a merely 'symbolic' meaning: the mother in it means the unattainable, which must be renounced in the interests of civilization; the father who is killed in the Oedipus myth is the 'inner' father, from whom one must set oneself free in order to become independent. (Freud, 1914a, p. 62)

In the other article Freud (1914b) took issue with Jung's dissent from his account of Schreber's schizophrenia in terms of regression from love of others to narcissistic self-love and sexual desire (see pp. 79–81 above).

Details of Jung's subsequent development of analytical psychology can be found in, for instance, his book *Modern Man in Search of a Soul*, and in his very readable and engaging autobiography, Memoirs, Dreams, Reflections. I have also written more about Jung in a couple of books, *Divine Therapy* and *Freud's Art*.

> *SUMMARY:* Although Jung contributed significantly to the development of psychoanalysis in its early years, his abandonment of Freud's sexual theory was followed by their friendship ending in December 1912, after which Jung developed a spiritually minded alternative to psychoanalysis which he called analytical psychology.

SEX AND REPRESSION

In view of Freud's break with Jung over the importance accorded sex in psychoanalysis, it is perhaps no surprise that, soon after this break, Freud (1915a) began consolidating psychoanalysis with an essay about sex. Previously he had emphasized variations in the object and aim of the sexual instinct (see p. 48 above). To these variations he now added, in the first of five metapsychology essays, variation in the pressure and force of the sexual instinct.

He also reiterated in this essay his previously stated argument concerning a distinction between the self-preserving ego instincts of hunger and thirst and the sexual instinct. This included noting variations in the sexual instinct. Examples included reversal of forms of this instinct into its opposite, as in the examples of sadism reversing into masochism, and voyeurism reversing into exhibitionism.

From this aspect of the sexual instinct Freud turned to the antitheses of 'loving-hating', 'loving-being loved', and 'loving and hating *vs.* indifference'. From all this and more he concluded in this metapsychology essay, 'Instincts and their vicissitudes', that variations in the instincts involve the 'biological' polarity of 'activity-passivity', the 'real' polarity of 'ego-external world', and the 'economic' polarity of 'pleasure-unpleasure' (Freud 1915a, pp. 133, 140).

This is hard to follow. So too is Freud's second metapsychology essay. In it he focused not on instincts but on repression. Previously he had called repression 'the cornerstone on which the whole structure of psycho-analysis rests' (Freud, 1914a, p. 16). Now, in this essay, he distinguished two types of repression: 'primal' repression preventing instinctual material ever becoming conscious; and repression 'proper', which stops once conscious 'derivatives' of this instinctual material remaining conscious (Freud, 1915b, pp. 147, 148).

In the early years of psychoanalysis Freud had explored manifestations of what is repressed and unconscious in the form of dreams, slips, jokes, neurotic symptoms, free associations, and in the form of the patient's transference experience of the psychoanalyst. He now famously described these manifestations of the unconscious as 'indications of a return of the repressed' (Freud, 1915b, p. 154).

Contrary to the widespread use of the term 'subconscious' interchangeably with the term 'unconscious', Freud dismissed the term 'subconscious' as 'incorrect' and 'misleading' (Freud, 1915b, p. 173). Banishing the term 'subconscious' from his writing, he wrote in terms of a distinction between unconscious, preconscious, and conscious mental processes. Whereas repressed unconscious mental processes are not accessible to the conscious mind, this is not true of preconscious mental processes, which are accessible to the conscious mind. A trite example is my preconscious awareness of what I had for breakfast today, about which I can easily become conscious provided I turn my attention to this preconscious awareness from which I can readily consciously recall what I then ate and drank.

Freud pictured what he described as the topographical arrangement of unconscious, preconscious, and conscious mental processes in terms of an analogy, of which he said,

> Let us therefore compare the system of the unconscious to a large entrance hall, in which the mental impulses jostle one another like separate individuals. Adjoining this entrance hall there is a second, narrower, room – a kind of drawing-room – in which consciousness, too, resides. But on the threshold between these two rooms a watchman performs his function: he examines the different mental impulses, acts as a censor, and will not admit them into the drawing-room if they displease him. [...] The impulses in the entrance hall of the unconscious are out of sight of the conscious, which is in the other room; to begin with they must remain unconscious. If they have already pushed their way forward to the threshold and have

> been turned back by the watchman, then they are inadmissible to consciousness: we speak of them as *repressed*. But even the impulses which the watchman has allowed to cross the threshold are not on that account necessarily conscious as well; they can only become so if they succeed in catching the eye of consciousness. We are therefore justified in calling this second room the system of the *preconscious*. In that case becoming conscious retains its purely descriptive sense. For any particular impulse, however, the vicissitude of repression consists in its not being allowed by the watchman to pass from the system of the unconscious into that of the preconscious. It is the same watchman whom we get to know as resistance when we try to lift the repression by means of the analytic treatment. (Freud, 1915–1917, pp. 295–296, italics in original).

What is repressed by the watchman or ego can only become conscious through experiencing its 'memory-trace'. Repressed instincts or drives cannot themselves become conscious, Freud insisted. They can, however, discharge their energy in the form of unconscious ideas or emotions, and they can become conscious in the form of 'anxiety' (Freud, 1915b, pp. 176, 179).

Examples for Freud included 'anxiety hysteria' – a term he used to describe the experience of being anxious without knowing what one is anxious about (Freud, 1915b, p. 182). He also pointed out that anxiety can be attached to a substitute for a repressed and unconscious idea. This can be illustrated with his patient Hans, suffering with anxiety due, Freud speculated, to his wanting his father to be dead, thus causing Hans to want to cuddle for comfort with his mother (see p. 64 above).

> *SUMMARY:* Between 1915 and 1917 Freud consolidated and added to his previous psychoanalytic theory about the instincts and their repression. In doing so he added to his previous account of unconscious-conscious dynamics a topographical model of the mind divided between repressed unconscious content and material in the preconscious mind available to conscious awareness.

17

FREUDIAN SYMBOLS

In founding psychoanalysis Freud used free association rather than symbols in interpreting dreams (see p. 30 above). During his close involvement with Jung, however, he added many examples of dream symbols to the 1909 and 1911 edition of his book *The Interpretation of Dreams*. By the time its 1914 edition was published, he had accumulated so many examples of dream symbols he devoted a whole new section of the book to them.

Armed with this increasing willingness to accord symbols an important place in psychoanalysis, Freud reinterpreted Breuer's account of his patient Anna O's hysterically paralysed arm and its psychologically traumatic cause (see p. 10 above). In doing so he wrote,

> Anyone who reads the history of [the Anna O] case now in the light of the knowledge gained in the last twenty years will at once perceive the [phallic] symbolism in it – the snakes, the stiffening, the paralysis of the arm – and, on taking into account the situation at the bedside of the young woman's sick father, will easily guess the real interpretation of her symptoms; his opinion of the part played by sexuality in her mental life will therefore be very different from that of her doctor.
> (Freud, 1914a, pp. 11–12)

To this Freud added attention to what has been described as schizophrenic use of concrete symbols in reducing them to what they symbolize. 'In putting on his stockings, for instance', Freud said of one patient with schizophrenia, 'he was disturbed by the idea that he must pull apart the stitches in the knitting, i.e. the holes, and to him every hole was a symbol of the female genital aperture'. Freud attributed this to schizophrenic abandonment of 'object-cathexes' – involvement with other people – in favour of overinvolvement in, or attachment to words and things (Freud, 1915c, pp. 200, 201).

He went on to devote an entire chapter of his 1915–1917 book, *Introductory Lectures on Psycho-Analysis*, to symbolism in dreams. This included listing numerous symbols of the vagina or uterus as '*pits, cavities* and *hollows* [...] *vessels* and *bottles* [...] *receptacles, boxes, trunks, cases, chests, pockets* [...] *cupboards, stoves* [...] *rooms* [...] [*d*]*oors* and *gates*'. He also listed symbols of the breasts as '*apples, peaches*, and *fruit*' (Freud, 1915–1917, p.156, italics in original).

Pride of place, however, was accorded by Freud in this chapter to symbols of male sexuality, specifically to symbols of the penis. After all, he insisted, the penis is the 'more striking and for both sexes the more interesting component of the genitals'. So saying he went on to illustrate, as instances of such symbols, now known as Freudian symbols, the following examples:

> [T]hings that resemble [the penis] in shape – things, accordingly, that are long and up-standing, such as *sticks, umbrellas, posts, trees* and so on [...] objects which share with the [penis] [...] the characteristic of penetrating into the body and injuring – thus, sharp *weapons* of every kind, *knives, daggers, spears, sabres*, but also fire-arms, *rifles, pistols* and *revolvers* [...] [T]he male organ can be replaced by objects from which water flows – *water-taps, watering-cans*, or *fountains* – or again by other objects which are capable of being lengthened, such as *hanging-lamps, extensible pencils*, etc. A no less obvious aspect of the organ explains the fact that *pencils, pen-holders, nail-files, hammers*, and other *instruments* are undoubted sexual symbols. The remarkable characteristic of the male organ which enables it to rise up in defiance of the laws of gravity, one of the phenomena of erection, leads to its being represented symbolically by *balloons, flying-machines* and most

recently by *Zeppelin airships*. (Freud, 1915–1917, pp.154–155, italics in original)

Not content with this long list of symbols for the penis, Freud added more. They included reptiles, fish, snakes, hats, and, surprisingly perhaps, overcoats.

All these objects, of course, have a use apart from any value they might have as symbols of the penis. Hence the quip 'Sometimes a cigar is just a cigar', coined apparently in 1950 by the writer Allen Wheelis, alluding to Freud's well-known addiction to smoking this form of tobacco.

In the following years the psychoanalyst Hanna Segal used the example of a Freudian phallic symbol to illustrate different uses of a violin as symbol of the penis. She did this with the help of the hypothetical example of two patients, A and B, of whom she said,

> [A] was once asked by his doctor why he had stopped playing the violin since his illness. He replied with some violence, 'Why? do you expect me to masturbate in public?' Another patient, B, dreamed one night that he and a young girl were playing a violin duet. He had associations to fiddling, masturbating, etc., from which it emerged clearly that the violin represented his genital and playing the violin represented a masturbation phantasy of a relation with the girl. (Segal, 1957, p. 49)

Segal interpreted the contrast between these two patients in terms of the schizophrenic patient A, equating the violin with the penis while patient B simply associated one as symbol of the other.

Prior to this, the psychoanalyst Jacques Lacan (1955–1956) had characterized schizophrenia or psychosis as involving the collapse of symbols into what they symbolize. He called it the collapse of the signifier onto the signified. Either way, it militates, he said, against talking cure psychoanalysis being applicable to the treatment of schizophrenic or psychotic states of mind.

Writing further about phallic symbolism, Lacan said in a passage symptomatic of what some readers like myself find virtually impossible to understand

> The phallus is the privileged signifier of that mark in which the role of the logos is joined with the advent of desire. It can be said that this signifier is chosen because it is the most tangible element in the real of sexual copulation, and also the most symbolic in the literal (typographical) sense of the term, since it is equivalent there to the (logical) copula. It might also be said that, by virtue of its turgidity, it is the image of the vital flow as it is transmitted in generation. (Lacan, 1958, p. 287)

More readily comprehensible is Lacan's claim that the phallus is a prime symbol of the patriarchal structuring of society, past and present (of which more on p. 167 below).

SUMMARY: Despite initially rejecting symbols as relevant to dream interpretation, Freud accorded considerable attention in his subsequent writing to sexual symbols, especially to phallic symbols of the penis, as have his followers, notably Lacan.

MORE ABOUT SEX

As well as consolidating and expanding his account of sexual symbols in his 1915–1917 book, *Introductory Lectures on Psycho-Analysis*, Freud also consolidated and expanded in this book on claims he had made in his 1905 book, *Three Essays on the Theory of Sexuality*.

These claims included noting, as follows, ways in which the infant's sexuality is shaped by those who first mother it of which Freud said:

> A child's intercourse with anyone responsible for his care affords him an unending source of sexual excitation and satisfaction from his erotogenic zones. This is especially so since the person in charge of him, who, after all, is as a rule his mother, herself regards him with feelings that are derived from her own sexual life: she strokes him, kisses him, rocks him and quite clearly treats him as a substitute for a complete sexual object. (Freud, 1905b, p. 223)

Freud also noted other ways in which the sexual preoccupations of parents and others shape their interaction with young children. Examples include his noting the following conversation between four-year-old Hans and his mother when, after his bath, she powdered around his penis, taking care not to touch it.

> Hans: Why don't you put your finger there?
> Mother: Because that'd be piggish.
> Hans: What's that? Piggish? Why?
> Mother: Because it's not proper.
> Hans: (laughing) But it's great fun.
> (Freud, 1905b, p. 19)

In addition Freud pointed out that the sex talk of other boys shapes the psychosexual development of the boy on the verge of puberty with the ensuing result.

> He begins to desire his mother herself in the sense with which he has recently become acquainted, and to hate his father anew as a rival who stands in the way of this wish; he comes, as we say, under the dominance of the Oedipus complex. He does not forgive his mother for having granted the favour of sexual intercourse not to himself but to his father, and he regards it as an act of unfaithfulness. If these impulses do not quickly pass, there is no outlet for them other than to run their course in phantasies which have as their subject his mother's sexual activities under the most diverse circumstances; and the consequent tension leads particularly readily to his finding relief in masturbation. (Freud, 1910d, p. 171)

Of the precursors of this complex in the three- or four-year-old boy, Freud said in his 1915–1917 *Introductory Lectures on Psycho-Analysis*,

> [I]t is easy to see that the little man wants to have his mother all to himself, that he feels the presence of his father as a nuisance, that he is resentful if his father indulges in any signs of affection towards his mother and that he shows satisfaction when his father has gone on a journey or is absent. He will often express his feelings directly in words and promise his mother to marry her. (Freud, 1915–1917, p. 332)

Rejecting the term Electra complex (a term used by Jung in, for instance, his 1913 essay, 'Psychoanalysis and neurosis'), Freud emphasized the similarity of the little girl's Oedipus complex to that of the boy in saying,

> Things happen in just the same way with little girls, with the necessary changes; an affectionate attachment to her father, a need to get rid of her mother as superfluous and to take her place, a coquetry which already employs the methods of later womanhood – these offer a charming picture, especially in small girls, which makes us forget the possibly grave consequences lying behind this infantile situation. (Freud, 1915–1917, p. 333)

Without expanding on what these grave consequences might entail, Freud went on to note ways in which parents contribute to their children's Oedipus complex. '[W]here there are several children', he maintained, 'the father will give the plainest evidence of his greater affection for his little daughter and the mother for her son' (Freud, 1915–1917, p. 333).

In subsequent years psychoanalysts paid much more attention to ways in which parents and others shape the psychology of infants and young children. The harmful psychological effects on infants of being evacuated away from their mothers during the 1939–1945 World War were followed by the psychoanalyst Donald Winnicott (1945), emphasizing the importance for the infant of the responsiveness of its mother to its psychological wishes and needs. This was followed by the psychoanalyst John Bowlby's much quoted observation:

> [W]hat is believed to be essential for mental health is that an infant and young child should experience a warm, intimate, and continuous relationship with his mother (or permanent mother-substitute – one person who steadily 'mothers' him) in which both find satisfaction and enjoyment. (Bowlby, 1953, p. 13)

Since then a great deal has been written by psychoanalysts and others about the importance of the responsive attachment of the primary caregiver to the infant for its future mental health. Examples include articles by the psychoanalyst Peter Fonagy (e.g. 2001), the psychologists Colwyn Trevarthen and Kenneth Aitken (2001), and the psychiatrist Jeremy Holmes (2015).

Psychoanalytic attachment theory has tended to go along with neglect of ways in which, whether or not they are sexually abused, infants and young children are affected by the more or less implicit and unconscious sexual messages conveyed to them by adults. Recently, however, there has been a revival, in a sense, of Freud's 1896 seduction theory and its attention to ways in which the infant's and the young child's psychology is shaped by the sexual response to them of those with whom they interact (see pp. 19–26 above).

This revival has been brought about not least by the psychoanalyst Jean Laplanche (1999). As well as noting Freud's (1905b) observation that the infant's bodily processes awaken sexual experience in its caregiver (see p. 106 above), Laplanche argued that all children are seduced consciously or unconsciously into taking on and being affected by the more or less puzzling sexually meaningful messages – he called them enigmatic signifiers – conveyed to them by parents and others.

Influenced by Laplanche, the psychoanalyst Mary Target (2007) argues that the infant's experience of sexuality is shaped by its mother responding differently to it depending on whether they see its behaviour as sexual or not. She reports evidence showing that, while mothers say they smile and laugh in response to seeing their infants smile and laugh, they look away in response to seeing their infants enjoying touching their genitals. The psychoanalyst Björn Salomonsson (2012) provides similar evidence in seeking to counter neglect – due, in his view, to psychoanalytic attachment theory – of ways in which the sexual experience evoked by infants in parents and others shape their responses to them.

> *SUMMARY:* In and following publication of his 1905 book about sex, Freud mentioned ways in which the sexual response of parents to infants shapes the latter's sexuality, not least their

Oedipus complex, about which Freud wrote in his 1915–1917 *Introductory Lectures on Psycho-Analysis*. This has been somewhat overlooked in post-Freudian attachment theory but attended to more recently thanks not least to the work of the psychoanalyst Jean Laplanche.

19

SYMPTOM FORMATION

As well as adding more about sex to his 1915–1917 *Introductory Lectures on Psycho-Analysis*, Freud added a critique of psychiatry. In doing so he deplored psychiatric accounts of symptom formation. He characterized them as describing 'mental disorders' and 'collecting them into clinical entities' without paying attention to their 'origin' or 'relation to each other' (Freud, 1915–1917, p. 20).

This is also true of the recent fifth edition of the *Diagnostic and Statistical Manual of Mental Disorders* (*DSM-5*) published by the American Psychiatric Association. It provides no information about the relation of mental disorders to each other. Nor, except in the case of organic disorders (such as dementia) or post-traumatic stress disorder (PTSD), does it say anything about the cause of mental or psychological problems or disorders.

Freud, by contrast, forged a causal account of them. He argued that they result from psychological conflict, leading to the patient regressing to fixation points in their early psychosexual development.

He maintained that this can also occur in sexual perversions, a point he illustrated with the case of a foot-and-shoe fetishist of whom he said,

> [He] can be plunged into irresistible sexual excitement only by a foot of a particular form wearing a shoe. He can recall an event from his sixth year which was decisive for the fixation of his libido. He was sitting on a stool beside the governess who was to give him lessons in English. The governess, who was an elderly, dried-up, plain-looking spinster, with pale-blue eyes and a snub nose, had something wrong with her foot that day, and on that account kept it, wearing a velvet slipper, stretched out on a cushion. Her leg itself was most decently concealed. A thin, scraggy foot, like the one he had then seen belonging to his governess, thereupon became (after a timid attempt at normal sexual activity at puberty) his only sexual object; and the man was irresistibly attracted if a foot of this kind was associated with other features besides which recalled the type of the English governess. (Freud, 1915–1917, p. 348)

Such perversions are the negative, said Freud, of neurosis resulting from repression and disguise of its fixated early psychosexual cause. Examples included Dora's nervous cough, which he diagnosed as resulting from sexual conflict in her teenage years leading to regression of her libido to the fixated and repressed oral stage of her psychosexual development, this being manifested by her persistent thumbsucking as a young child (see p. 58 above).

Another example was Ernst Lanzer. Freud (1909b) attributed his symptoms at least in part to conflict between unconscious hatred and conscious love of his father involving fixation of his libido at the anal stage of his psychosexual development (see p. 73 above).

To this case study Freud (1911b) added the claim that Schreber's paranoia was caused by conflict about his homosexual desire involving regression to the narcissistic stage of his psychosexual development. His symptoms were due, said Freud, to his defensively repressing, reversing, and projecting narcissistic sexual desire for men like himself onto his doctor, Flechsig. It was this, Freud argued, that caused Schreber's paranoid delusion that his body was being changed into a woman to enable Flechsig to sexually abuse and persecute him (see p. 80 above).

Publication of this case study was preceded by publication of Freud's (1909a) account of four-year-old Hans's horse phobia. He interpreted it as resulting from Hans's Oedipal wish to sleep with his mother through his father being dead and gone (see pp. 65–68 above). Freud (1923b) later described such a wish as heterosexual and positive. He contrasted it with what he described as the inverted or negative homosexual Oedipal wish of Sergei Pankejeff to take his mother's place in sexual intercourse with his father (see p. 88 above).

'[T]he Oedipus complex may justly be regarded as the nucleus of the neuroses', Freud declared in his *Introductory Lectures on Psycho-Analysis* (Freud, 1915–1917, p. 337). To this Freud (1920b) added the example of an eighteen-year-old patient, Margarethe Csonka, whose neurotic symptoms, including a suicide attempt, he attributed to revival of her Oedipus complex by her parents having another child when she was sixteen.

SUMMARY: Freud attributed symptom formation in neurosis, which he described as the negative of perversion, to conflict causing regression to fixated and repressed oral, anal, genital, narcissistic, or Oedipal stages in their early psychosexual development.

PSYCHOANALYTIC TREATMENT

Fundamental to the basics of Freud is his legacy of psychoanalytic treatment. Unlike psychiatrists then and now who prescribe medication, produced by drug companies, to relieve symptoms of mental ill-health, Freud sought to relieve his patients of their symptoms by enabling them to become conscious of these symptoms' repressed and unconscious cause.

TREATMENT METHODS

Central to Freud's treatment methods was his use of a free association development of the pressure technique which he used in the 1890s in treating Lucy R and Elisabeth von R (see p. 13 above). He called it 'the fundamental rule of psycho-analysis' (Freud, 1914a, p. 147). It involves requiring psychoanalytic patients to say whatever occurs to them, however disagreeable, nonsensical, unimportant, or irrelevant it might seem.

Corresponding to this rule is Freud's recommendation that, in conducting psychoanalytic treatment, psychoanalysts should adopt a stance of evenly suspended attention. Explaining this stance, he said,

> [I]t rejects the use of any special expedient (even that of taking notes). It consists in not directing one's notice to anything in particular and in maintaining the same 'evenly-suspended attention' (as I have called it) in the face of all that one hears. In this way we spare ourselves a strain on our attention which could not in any case be kept up for several hours daily, and we avoid a danger which is inseparable from the exercise of deliberate attention. For as soon as anyone deliberately concentrates his attention to a certain degree, he begins to select from the material before him; one point will be fixed in his mind with particular clearness and some other will be correspondingly disregarded, and in making this selection he will be following his expectations or inclinations. (Freud, 1912b, pp. 111–112)

In addition to the treatment methods of free association and evenly suspended attention, Freud recommended offering patients who applied for psychoanalytic treatment an initial two-week period of treatment to determine whether they would benefit from it. For each patient he took on for treatment, he assigned the same hour every day of the week except Sundays and holidays.

He also warned patients that their treatment might take six months or more: Dora ended her treatment three months after it began; Ernst Lanzer's treatment lasted less than a year; and Sergei Pankejeff's treatment continued for over four years. Why so long? Because of 'the slowness with which deep-going changes in the mind are accomplished', Freud explained (Freud, 1913a, p. 130).

Freud moreover insisted that his patients pay for their treatment. After all, it was the way he earned his living. Furthermore, by paying for their treatment, patients were motivated to bring it to 'an end' as soon as possible (Freud, 1913a, p. 132).

Unlike Jung, who treated patients face to face, Freud required his patients to lie on a couch while he sat out of sight behind them. He could not bear being 'stared at by people for eight hours a day (or more)', he explained. He also did not want the expression on his face to influence what his patients told him, or influence their 'transference' onto him of their more or less unconscious experience of other significant people in their lives (Freud, 1913a, p. 134).

This was in keeping with his recommendation that psychoanalysts reveal as little as possible about themselves so as to remain a blank screen or tabula rasa on which they could project their transference experience. This experience is a crucial element of psychoanalytic treatment because, he maintained, it makes the patient's repressed and unconscious 'impulses immediate and manifest' (Freud, 1912b, p. 108).

Only when the patient has formed 'an effective transference' or 'proper *rapport*' with the psychoanalyst, he insisted, should the unconscious cause of their ills be interpreted (Freud, 1913a, p. 139). As well as providing examples in his long case studies of patients transferring previous experience onto him (see, for instance, p. 73 above), Freud illustrated the transference with the following examples:

> [T]he patient does not say that he remembers that he used to be defiant and critical towards his parents' authority; instead, he behaves in that way to the doctor. He does not remember how he came to a helpless and hopeless deadlock in his infantile sexual researches; but he produces a mass of confused dreams and associations, complains that he cannot succeed in anything and asserts that he is fated never to carry through what he undertakes. He does not remember having been intensely ashamed of certain sexual activities and afraid of their being found out; but he makes it clear that he is ashamed of the treatment on which he is now embarked and tries to keep it secret from everybody. (Freud, 1914a, p. 150)

Herein, argued Freud, resides material on which the psychoanalyst can base an interpretation or explanation to the patient of the unconscious cause of their problems. Interpretations should not, he warned, take the form of 'lightning diagnoses'. The interpretation should be well timed and only delivered when the patient is 'already so close to it that he has only one short step more to make in order to get hold of the explanation for himself' (Freud, 1913a, p. 140).

In addition to providing examples of psychoanalytic interpretations in his published case studies (see e.g. pp. 66, 74 above), Freud provided the following hypothetical example in which the psychoanalyst tells the patient,

> Up to your *n*th year you regarded yourself as the sole and unlimited possessor of your mother; then came another baby and brought you grave disillusionment. Your mother left you for some time, and even after her reappearance she was never again devoted to you exclusively. Your feelings towards your mother became ambivalent, your father gained a new importance for you (Freud, 1937b, p. 261)

Testing the validity of such interpretations includes attending to whether it tallies with what the patient subsequently says and does. There is, however, a problem with this 'Tally Argument', as it has been called (Smith, 2003, p. 34). For it is perfectly possible that what the patient says or does following an interpretation is due not to its validity but to its suggestive effect.

Freud warned psychoanalysts about the problem of suggestion. He also warned them to beware of the countertransference feelings evoked in them by their patient's transference experience of them. This was particularly the case after Jung acted on his countertransference reaction to his patient Sabina Spielrein's falling in love with him by having an affair with her.

To minimize the risk of psychoanalysts acting on their countertransference feelings, Freud issued the following emphatically worded recommendation:

> I cannot advise my colleagues too urgently to model themselves during psycho-analytic treatment on the surgeon who puts aside all his feelings even his human sympathy, and concentrates his mental forces on the single aim of performing the operation as skilfully as possible. [...] The justification for requiring this emotional coldness in the analyst is that it creates the most advantageous conditions for both parties: for the doctor a desirable protection for his own emotional life and for the patient the largest amount of help that we can give him to-day. (Freud, 1912c, p. 115)

In addition, Freud recommended that to help psychoanalysts guard against countertransference feelings for their patients, they should identify these feelings by continuing their self-analysis after their training was complete.

PSYCHOANALYSIS TODAY

Nowadays, in part to help psychoanalysts master their countertransference feelings, they are psychoanalysed prior to, during, and often after they finish their psychoanalytic training. Unlike in Freud's time, however, psychoanalysts today are encouraged not to try to abolish their countertransference experience of their patients. Rather, they are encouraged to pay attention to it because, as the psychoanalyst Paula Heimann (1950) was one of the first to point out, it provides valuable information about the patient.

Furthermore, unlike Freud who, before the 1914–1918 World War, treated patients six days a week, today's psychoanalysts treat each of their patients for at most five daily fifty-minute appointments each week.

Otherwise, the treatment approach adopted by today's psychoanalysts is very similar to that forged by Freud. This approach is particularly helpfully explained by the psychoanalyst Jane Milton and her colleagues, not least through case examples. They explain the interplay of transference, countertransference, and interpretation in psychoanalytic treatment with various illustrations including the following:

> Mark, who was very stuck and restricted in his life, would come to a session enthusiastic about a possible new job, and his analyst would feel pleased for them both that things were moving. Then over the following days he would lapse into passivity, mentioning vaguely that he had forgotten to phone for the job application, or had lost it. The analyst found herself disappointed and restless, wanting to prod Mark into action, and would notice she was making slightly bossy sounding comments about his inaction. He would become more passive while she would become more active, all the time trying to hide her irritation. At times she would find a sharp edge entered her voice, in

> spite of her efforts to go on thinking and containing. In response, Mark would sound a mixture of meek and subtly mocking. It would start just a bit to resemble the sado-masochistic way Mark and his authoritarian father related to each other. The analyst needed to find a way of reflecting to herself about this situation. She had to get outside her own feelings and impulses, and be able to observe the whole situation. Only then could she make an interpretation that engaged Mark's curiosity, showed her understanding of his situation and had a chance of helping him to alter rather than just go on repeating a lifelong pattern. (Milton et al., 2011, pp. 14–15)

Milton and her colleagues also indicate that, more than Freud, they focus on enabling patients to become aware of their 'inner world' involving their 'superego' and other examples of their internalization of their experience of others as 'object relations' figures within their minds. (This is in accordance with an aspect of psychoanalysis which I explain further in Chapter 24). In addition, in keeping with the argument developed by the psychoanalyst Wilfred Bion in relation to schizophrenia (see p. 82 above), Milton and her colleagues illustrate the 'containment' by psychoanalysts of their patients' projected feelings (Milton et al., 2011, pp. 20, 29, 63).

More than in Freud's time, psychoanalytic treatment today often involves focus *not only* on the patient's transference experience of the psychoanalyst and on the psychoanalyst's countertransference experience of the patient *but also* on the relation between these two forms of experience in what has been described as 'the analytic third' (Ogden, 1994, p. 3). This together with Bowlby's attachment theory (see pp. 108–109 above) and its subsequent development also very much influences the work of many psychoanalysts today.

Whether or not it incorporates these developments, psychoanalytic treatment has been assessed as effective by several large-scale studies (see e.g. Fonagy, 2015). But full-scale, five-times-a-week, long-term psychoanalytic psychotherapy (LTPP) costs £8,000 to £14,000 a year. Patients receiving less frequent psychoanalytic treatment can expect to pay £50 to £120 for each fifty-minute appointment.

Moreover, in Britain, full-scale LTPP is scarcely available outside London and a few other major cities. Something similar is probably true of other countries in which LTPP is practiced.

SHORT-TERM PSYCHOANALYTIC PSYCHOTHERAPY (STPP)

One solution to the problem posed by the expense in time and money and relative lack of availability of LTPP is its provision on a short-term, once-a-week, low-fee, voluntary, or, in Britain, on a National Health Service (NHS) basis. Like LTPP, STPP usually consists of fifty-minute appointments. Instead of the patient lying on a couch with the psychoanalyst sitting behind them, however, the patient and therapist usually sit face to face.

Unlike LTPP which, with Freud's free association method, can go every which way, STPP is more focused, with the psychoanalytic psychotherapist adopting a more active stance than the evenly suspended approach advocated by Freud (see pp. 114–115 above). The focus of each patient's STPP may well be rather different from the Oedipus complex focus of Freud's psychoanalytic treatment of, for instance, four-year-old Hans. Today, the focus of STPP treatment is decided during and following the patient's initial appointments.

These appointments begin with an assessment of whether the patient is likely to benefit from STPP. It includes learning from the patient about their childhood and subsequent life history. It may also include asking the patient to recall their earliest memory and a recent dream, and learning whether they can use a transference interpretation based on some of this data.

Interpretations during STPP treatment often take the form recommended by the psychoanalytically minded psychiatrist David Malan (1963). This involves a triangle of interpretation in which the patient's past and present experience of significant people in their lives is linked with their experience of the psychotherapist.

Examples of STPP include the following from the psychoanalytic psychotherapist Alex Coren describing a patient, Chris, of whom Coren says,

> [He] was a highly impulsive, labile and attention-seeking young man whose father had been malignly neglectful and disinterested while his mother was experienced by Chris as more benign but as very intrusive. Chris had a history of taking regular overdoses leading to hospitalization and regularly missed sessions. After one such occasion, shortly after beginning treatment, Chris thought he would apply to become an ambulance driver. Two issues dominated his treatment. In relation to his missed sessions (and symbolically his overdose attempts) should the therapist intervene like his intrusive, if benign, mother, or not respond at all and risk becoming like Chris' neglectful, and malign father? Equally the issue of Chris' interest in becoming an ambulance driver shortly after taking an overdose could be seen as reflecting two different parts of himself – a self-destructive one and a life-affirming one. Which of these were being brought to therapy? These were used as generic foci for the treatment. (Coren, 2009, p. 145)

Illustrations of STPP are also provided in a book by Simon Cregeen. It includes the case of a young girl, Lucinda. After her first appointment at a centre treating young people suffering with depression, she did not return. During the next eighteen months she truanted from school, spent a lot of time in bed or in her room, lost touch with her friends, cut herself, and felt she was rubbish. She then returned, aged fourteen, to the centre where she was again assessed and provided with twenty-eight once-weekly treatment appointments while her parents were offered seven separate supportive appointments.

Similar provision was made for a fifteen-year-old, Sam, and his refugee single-parent mother. Following his serious overdose with paracetamol and alcohol, the centre formulated the following assessment of his difficulties:

> Sam is struggling with his sexual identification as an adolescent male. He wishes for heterosexual intimacy but fears rejection. He is conflicted in his loyalty to his mother and struggles with low self-esteem and anxiety [...] His peers' developmental progress into sexual relationships has left him behind and challenged his sense of self and potency. He has unresolved loss and rage in relation to his father which in turn affects his masculine identification. This loss

> may be compounded by intergenerational trauma and loss affecting his ability to individuate, as separation would be perceived as abandonment of his mother [...] His defence mechanisms have entailed manic denial (being one of the lads in a drunken, noisy group), projection and aggression. (Cregeen, 2017, p. 49)

STPP seems, at least from the findings of Paul Knekt (2008) and his colleagues, to produce benefits more quickly than LTPP during the first year of treatment. LTPP was, however, found in this study to be more effective than STPP at three-year follow-up.

Freud was sceptical about short- or at least fixed-term psychoanalytic treatment, of which he said,

> I have [...] employed this fixing of a time-limit [...] and I have also taken the experiences of other analysts into account. There can be only one verdict about the value of this blackmailing device: it is effective provided that one hits the right time for it. But it cannot guarantee to accomplish the task completely. On the contrary, we may be sure that, while part of the material will become accessible under the pressure of the threat, another part will be kept back and thus become buried, as it were, and lost to our therapeutic efforts. (Freud, 1937a, p. 218)

It is therefore unlikely that Freud would have approved of STPP.

He certainly did not approve of psychiatric treatment. He likened it to the 'external' approach adopted by medical research in histology in contrast to the focus of anatomy on 'the internal structure of the body', which he likened to psychoanalysis studying 'the internal mechanism of the mind' (Freud, 1915–1917, p. 255).

COGNITIVE BEHAVIOURAL THERAPY

Since Freud's time, psychoanalytic treatment has been, and continues to be contrasted unfavourably with cognitive behavioural therapy (CBT), which seeks to enable patients to manage their problems by changing their negative thoughts and behaviour. In Britain, since the introduction in 2008 of the Improving Access to Psychological

Therapies (IAPT) programme, CBT is much more widely available than psychoanalytic treatment within the NHS. Helpful guidelines for assessing the suitability of patients for this form of treatment are provided in an article by Paul Blenkiron (1999).

Interestingly, although CBT differs from psychoanalytic treatment – it focuses, for instance, more on the present than on the past – the effective ingredients of both forms of treatment are the same. At least this is the finding of an American researcher, Jonathan Shedler. He says of these ingredients,

> [They include] unstructured, open-ended dialogue (e.g., discussion of fantasies and dreams); identifying recurring themes in the patient's experience; linking the patient's feelings and perceptions to past experiences; drawing attention to feelings regarded by the patient as unacceptable (e.g., anger, envy, excitement); pointing out defensive maneuvers; interpreting warded-off or unconscious wishes, feelings, or ideas; focusing on the therapy relationship as a topic of discussion; and drawing connections between the therapy relationship and other relationships. (Shedler, 2010, pp. 103–104)

More recent investigation of the relative effectiveness of psychoanalytic treatment and CBT includes a study by the psychoanalyst Marianne Leuzinger-Bohleber (2019) and her colleagues. They report that three years after the long-term treatment of patients with chronic depression ended, those who had been treated psychoanalytically had significantly more structural change in their psychology than those treated with CBT.

SUMMARY: Freud's treatment methods – including free association, attention to the transference, and interpretation of the unconscious cause of the patient's psychological ills – continue, with some modifications, to inform long-term and short-term psychoanalytic treatment today, a method of treatment now often contrasted with cognitive behavioural therapy.

CONCLUSIONS TO PART IV

Freud's break with Jung in January 1913 was followed by Freud consolidating his previous psychoanalytic account of sex and repression. It was also followed by increased attention by Freud to what are now often referred to as Freudian phallic symbols, and by Freud adding to his account of psychosexual development observations about the Oedipus complex. To this, subsequent psychoanalysts have added attention, more than Freud, to attachment and other intersubjective factors. These include not least enigmatic or puzzling sexual meanings shaping our psychology. Long before that, in his 1915–1917 psychoanalytic lectures, Freud consolidated his psychoanalytic account of symptom formation, and his account of his method of psychoanalytic treatment which, with some modifications, is practiced today in long- or short-term form. Either way it is rather different from another current psychological treatment, namely cognitive behavioural therapy.

PART V
WAR AND ITS PSYCHOANALYTIC AFTERMATH

During and following the 1914–1918 World War, Freud transforms psychoanalysis. This includes the transformation and aftermath for us today resulting from his psychoanalyzing severe depression in terms of defensive identification with those who have been loved, hated, and lost. This is followed, in 1920, by his adding to his wish-fulfilling theory of the unconscious an account of death instinct-driven destructiveness in terms of which, paradoxically, he explains what would now be called the post-traumatic disorder suffered by victims of the war, and the repetitive *fort-da* game played by his eighteen-month-old grandson in managing separation from his mother. In 1923, Freud rejigs psychoanalysis by developing a new id-ego-superego theory of the mind. It results in an ego psychology and object relations version of psychoanalysis which is still very influential today.

MOURNING AND MELANCHOLIA

Six months after the start of the 1914–1918 World War, Freud wrote about its disillusioning effects. 'Not only is it more bloody and more destructive than any war of other days', he said of this war,

> [I]t is at least as cruel, as embittered, as implacable as any that has preceded it. [...] It tramples in blind fury on all that comes in its way, as though there were to be no future and no peace among men after it is over. It cuts all the common bonds between the contending peoples, and threatens to leave a legacy of embitterment that will make any renewal of those bonds impossible for a long time to come. (Freud, 1915e, pp. 278–279)

Embitterment and hatred also featured in Freud's essay 'Mourning and melancholia'. Like his essay about the disillusioning effects of the 1914–1918 World War, it too was written soon after the war began. Its final version, however, was published two years later. In it Freud likened mourning the death of someone one loves to the experience of the severe depression involved in melancholia. Both states of mind involve loss. And, he added, they are both marked by withdrawal of interest in the outside world.

In mourning this withdrawal is due, he argued, to preoccupation of the mourner with doing the grief work involved in detaching themselves 'bit by bit' from those they have lost (Freud, 1917, p. 245). Grief work can, however, get stuck. A fictional example is Miss Havisham in Charles Dickens's novel *Great Expectations*. Deserted by her fiancé on their wedding day, she continues to wear her wedding dress in seeming denial of his loss, and in the hope that he will return.

A real-life example of grief work becoming stuck is an elderly woman, Sheila, who I met through work on a book, *Freudian Tales*.

> More than three years after the death of her husband, she still had his and her name on her front door. After his cremation she could not bear to collect his ashes. Nor could she face being present when they were buried in the local cemetery. She could not bear others at Cruse, an organisation set up to help the bereaved, talk about the last moments of those they had lost. Over three years after her husband's death his dressing-gown still hung on the back of their bedroom door, and his shaving things were still on a shelf in the bathroom where his toothbrush, together with hers, was still in a rack. 'I suppose at the back of my mind it feels like perhaps he's just gone away and he's coming back', she told me. (Sayers, 1997, p. 177)

She had withdrawn from everything that did not relate to the husband she had lost through his death. If, by contrast, the grief work involved in mourning does not get stuck, it may well result in the mourner managing to detach themselves from persisting preoccupation with the person whose loss and death they grieve. This, said Freud, enables them to get involved and interested in the world around them again.

Familiar with psychoanalysis, the writer Alison Light says of her recovery, as one could call it, from mourning the death on 9 December 1996 of her husband, Raphael Samuel,

> Eventually the repeated repetitions, all those anniversaries counted in days, then weeks, then months and years, force one to register that the absence feels different, if only by being, like the pain, more familiar. However stymied the mourner feels inside, however inert, outside changes remorselessly. So, for example, the general election that May [1997] was a terrible wrench, an assault on my inwardness.
> (Light, 2019, p. 170)

No such revival from inwardness occurs in the case of the severely depressed melancholic. Or so Freud implied. Like the bereaved person in the initial stages of grief, the severely depressed melancholic responds to loss, he said, with persisting withdrawal of interest in the world around them. They remain beached in inwardness.

Unlike with the bereaved, it is not always clear, observed Freud, who or what the melancholic has lost. And, he added, quite differently from those whose withdrawal from the external world into inwardness is due to bereavement, melancholia is characterized by self-hatred.

Melancholics deride themselves, observed Freud, 'to a degree that finds utterance in self-reproaches and self-revilings, and culminates in a delusional expectation of punishment' (Freud, 1917, p. 244). Certainly this was true of Professor Brown:

> He loathed himself. Having gone on sick leave after suffering stage fright which prevented him giving one of his lectures because the theme touched too closely on a central issue in his life, he became so depressed he could not return to work. Instead he took early retirement. This exacerbated the problem. Loss of his job left him full of self-loathing. He hated himself for staying in bed all day, for drinking, for the state of his flat, for wearing the same filthy clothes day in, day out. He was consumed with guilt and became convinced that, because of his failure to pay a fine for a minor traffic offence, he would be punished with imprisonment.

Why does the melancholic, like Professor Brown, make such a meal of their self-contempt? Why do they go on and on about it to others? In doing so, argued Freud, melancholics split themselves in two. One part attacks and criticizes another part. One part – an ego ideal part – acts as judge. The other part is judged and found guilty.

Freud was struck by the observation that the part of themselves which the melancholic hates corresponds to someone in their life whom they have loved, hated, and lost. In the absence of ready case studies with which to illustrate this process, Freud described a general type of melancholic of whom he said,

> The woman who loudly pities her husband for being tied to such an incapable wife as herself is really accusing her husband of being incapable, in whatever sense she may mean this. There is no need to be greatly surprised that a few genuine self-reproaches are scattered among those that have been transposed back. These are allowed to obtrude themselves, since they help to mask the others and make recognition of the true state of affairs impossible. (Freud, 1917, p. 248)

What has happened here? By way of answer Freud argued that it results not from the defence of repression, reversal, or projection – defences which I have previously illustrated in this book. Rather, he maintained, the main defence in melancholia involves identification. The melancholic, he argued, defends against loss of, or disappointment – disillusion even – in those they both love and hate by identifying with them. They cast their 'shadow' on the melancholic's ego (Freud, 1917, p. 249).

Why does the melancholic resort to this defence of identification, also sometimes referred to as the defence of introjection? Because, said Freud, the melancholic's attachment to those they have loved, hated, and lost was formed on a narcissistic basis. Melancholia, he maintained, involves regression of the patient from love of others – 'object love' – to an early childhood stage of psychosexual development centred on narcissistic 'self-love' (Freud, 1917, pp. 249, 252).

But if melancholia involves narcissistic self-love, why does it sometimes end in suicide? Freud attributed this to the melancholic feeling so overwhelmed by the part of the ego identified with the hated aspect of those they have loved and lost they paradoxically kill themselves – the bad and hated aspect of their ego – to save ego's good and loved aspect.

Extreme cases can involve the psychotic delusion of being inhited by an evil figure which threatens to do dreadful damage to others as well as to the melancholic themselves. It can even tragically eventuate in the melancholic killing themselves and others to protect them all from this evil figure, an outcome that has been called homicide-suicide (see e.g. Flynn et al., 2016).

Another, usually much less extreme and appalling outcome of melancholia is its alternation, in some cases, with hypomanic excitement. Once diagnosed as manic-depressive psychosis, its severe form is now diagnosed as Bipolar Disorder 1 with hypomanic symptoms including inflated self-esteem, decreased need for sleep, increased talkativeness, racing thoughts, and being easily distracted.

Peter, a man in his late fifties when I met him, is a case in point. Certainly his thoughts raced and he recalled grandiose manic delusions and dreams as he talked to me. Examples included a delusion or dream which he described to me,

> I came to this sort of void in space. No stars. Nothing. It had a sort of floor to it. Riveted. I was placed there. And something said to me, 'Now Peter. You have the power of God. Whether you have to wait here one, two, millions of years, you can live through it. You can cause a big bang and create a solar system. And start all over again. Then you'll have to pick the type of planet you want'. (Sayers, 1997 pp. 192–193)

Freud (1917) attributed the hypomanic excitement alternating with melancholia occurring in manic-depression to the regression to narcissistic self-preoccupation and self-love which he believed is involved in this condition. A more convincing account of the alternation of these two states of mind – hypomania and melancholia – is arguably the explanation provided by the psychoanalyst Melanie Klein.

On the basis of her pioneering psychoanalytic work with very young children, she argued that melancholia and milder forms of depression are due to loss reviving a depressive position state of mind occurring in early infancy. She characterized this state of mind as involving depressive fear in the infant lest, in attacking the mother it hates, it might have damaged and lost the mother it loves. If all goes well, it seeks to repair the harm done by hatred to its mother.

Klein (1935, 1940) contrasted this resolution of depression mobilized by loss with hypomania or mania. She regarded them as defence against depression and loss through denial of inner psychological feelings and of dependence on others, in the first place the mother, by instead omnipotently controlling and disparaging them.

Like Freud, as I have indicated, Klein was influenced by his relating depression to loss. Many others, psychoanalysts included, continue today to relate depression to loss. In doing so, many often incorporate the attention by the psychoanalyst John Bowlby (1969), and by many others such as the psychiatrist Jeremy Holmes (2015), to ways in which the outcome of loss is shaped by the security, or otherwise, of attachment to and from others, beginning in earliest infancy. Informed by these perspectives, long-term psychoanalytic therapy has been shown empirically by the psychoanalyst Peter Fonagy (2015) and his colleagues to be more effective than other approaches in helping those with treatment-resistant depression.

> *SUMMARY:* With his 1917 essay 'Mourning and melancholia', Freud not only highlighted the defence of identification involved in melancholia or severe depression. He also demonstrated a link between loss and depression subsequently attended to by Melanie Klein and also by John Bowlby and his followers dealing with ways in which reactions to loss are shaped by attachment, beginning in earliest infancy, to and from others.

TRAUMA AND THE DEATH INSTINCT

In his pre-psychoanalytic work Freud, together with Breuer, noted ways in which patients repeated psychological trauma they had suffered in their bodily symptoms of hysteria. Famous examples included Anna O repeating the trauma of seeing or hallucinating seeing a snake about to attack her sick father in the bodily symptom of paralysis of her right arm (see p. 10 above). '*Hysterics suffer mainly from reminiscences*', Breuer and Freud accordingly concluded (Breuer & Freud, 1893, p. 7, italics in original).

Some years later, Freud (1914a) described patients in psychoanalytic treatment remembering, repeating, and working through the otherwise repressed, unconscious, and more or less traumatic cause of their ills. Following the end of the 1914–1918 World War, he also noted, as did many others, ways in which soldiers relived the trauma they had suffered in the form of repeated nightmares, just as those suffering post-traumatic stress disorder (PTSD) do today.

Influenced by Freud, the psychiatrist W. H. R. Rivers diagnosed the repeated nightmares of his 1914–1918 World War army officer patients as due to nightmares breaking through their habit of repressing emotional upset first learnt when they went, as young children, to boarding school. (For further details of a similar phenomenon today, see *Boarding School Syndrome* by Joy Schaverien.)

Drawing on Freud's talking cure treatment method, Rivers sought to treat his war traumatized army officer patients by getting them to talk about the trauma they had suffered. Examples included a young officer who had been wounded during the war while extricating himself from earth in which he had been buried, of whom Rivers said,

> When he had recounted his symptoms and told me about his method of dealing with his disturbing thoughts I asked him to tell me candidly his own opinion concerning the possibility of keeping these obtrusive visitors from his mind. He said at once that it was obvious to him that memories such as those he had brought with him from the war could never be forgotten. Nevertheless, since he had been told by everyone that it was his duty to forget them he had done his utmost in this direction. I then told the patient my own views concerning the nature and treatment of his state. I agreed with him that such memories could not be expected to disappear from the mind and advised him no longer to try to banish them but that he should see whether it was not possible to make them into tolerable, if not even pleasant, companions instead of evil influences which forced themselves upon his mind whenever the silence and inactivity of the night came round. The possibility of such a line of treatment had never previously occurred to him, but my plan seemed reasonable and he promised to give it a trial. We talked about his war experiences and his anxieties, and following this he had the best night he had had for five months. (Rivers, 1918, n.p.)

It is not only victims of war who repeat the trauma they have suffered. So too, Freud pointed out, do patients in psychoanalytic treatment. They repeat early childhood traumas in their experience of their psychoanalysts. Examples included Freud's Rat Man patient, Ernst Lanzer, re-experiencing in relation to Freud his traumatic experience as a young child of his father's anger with him (see p. 73 above).

Writing generally about such patients, Freud said, 'they contrive once more to feel themselves scorned, to oblige the physician to speak severely to them and treat them coldly' (Freud, 1920a, p.21). To this Freud added the following illustrations:

> the benefactor who is abandoned in anger after a time by each of his *protégés*, however much they may otherwise differ from one another, and who thus seems doomed to taste all the bitterness of ingratitude; or the man whose friendships all end in betrayal by his friend; or the man who time after time in the course of his life raises someone else into a position of great private or public authority and then, after a certain interval, himself upsets that authority and replaces him by a new one; or, again, the lover each of whose love affairs with a woman passes through the same phases and reaches the same conclusion. (Freud, 1920a, p.22)

Freud argued that such symptoms are due to a repetition compulsion geared to repeating trauma so as to reduce their stimulating effect to zero. Likening this to the zero effect of stimuli on the dead, Freud depicted the repetition compulsion, perhaps rather strangely, as motivated by a death instinct.

Having arrived at this explanation of the repeated nightmares suffered by victims of the 1914–1918 World War, Freud went on to illustrate the compulsion to repeat trauma with a repeated game played by his eighteen-month-old grandson, Ernst, of whom he said,

> [Ernst had] an occasional disturbing habit of taking any small objects he could get hold of and throwing them away from him into a corner, under the bed, and so on, so that hunting for his toys and picking them up was often quite a business. As he did this he gave vent to a loud, long-drawn-out 'o-o-o-o', accompanied by an expression of interest and satisfaction. (Freud, 1920a, p.14).

Together with Ernst's mother, Sophie, Freud agreed that 'o-o-o-o' signified '*fort*' meaning 'gone'. This was confirmed for Freud by the following observation:

> [Ernst] had a wooden reel with a piece of string tied round it. It never occurred to him to pull it along the floor behind him, for instance, and play at its being a carriage. What he did was to hold the reel by the string and skilfully throw it over the edge of his curtained cot, so that it disappeared into it, at the same time uttering his expressive 'o-o-o-o'. He then pulled the reel out of the cot again by the string and hailed its reappearance with a joyful '*da*' [meaning 'there']. (Freud, 1920a, p.15)

It was evidently Ernst's way of managing the relatively minor trauma of his mother sometimes being absent, an event he symbolized by staging her departure and return with small objects and with sounds signifying their being first absent then present, first 'gone' and then 'here'.

Ernst also used his own absence to symbolize that of his mother. This became evident to Freud from an occasion of which he said

> [Sophie] had been away for several hours and on her return was met with the words 'Baby o-o-o-o!' which was at first incomprehensible. It soon turned out, however, that during this long period of solitude [Ernst] had found a method of making *himself* disappear. He had discovered his reflection in a full-length mirror which did not quite reach to the ground, so that by crouching down he could make his mirror-image 'gone'. (Freud, 1920a, p. 15, n.1 – italics in original)

With his repeated *fort-da* game, as it has been called, Freud argued, Ernst turned the 'passive' situation of being left by his mother into one in which he was the 'active' agent (Freud, 1920a, p. 16).

Or, as the psychoanalyst Jonathan Lear has put it: by interpreting Ernst's '*o-o-o-o*' and '*da*' sounds as meaning 'gone' and 'there', his mother and grandfather, Sophie and Freud, enabled him to use his otherwise 'disturbing habit' of throwing objects away as means of experiencing and thinking about 'loss' (Lear, 2000, p. 97). And, of course, the ability to give experience words is a precondition of thinking about loss and other matters in talking cure psychoanalysis.

Applied to cases of PTSD, this may involve relating recently occurring trauma to the patient's past experience. In her novel *The Eye in the Door* (1993), Pat Barker imagines the psychoanalytic talking cure treatment used by Rivers enabling a victim of the trauma of the 1914–1918 World War to relate his resulting nightmares to those he suffered as a young child. This is likewise the perspective sought by soldiers with PTSD today insofar as they seek psychoanalytic help because, as one observer notes, their traumatic military experience links with their 'earlier developmental and familial history' (Schechter, 2010, p. 1241).

SUMMARY: Freud attributed the repetition of trauma – not least the trauma suffered by victims of the 1914–1918 World War – to a death instinct motivated repetition compulsion. He illustrated this compulsion with the example of a repeated *fort-da* game played by his eighteen-month-old grandson, Ernst. He understood this as means by which Ernst managed the trauma of his mother sometimes being gone.

OEDIPUS, CASTRATION, PENIS ENVY

Freud added to his account of his eighteen-month-old grandson Ernst's *fort-da* game (see pp. 135–137 above) the possibility that it might have been a way of defiantly revenging himself on his mother for sometimes being absent from him by making objects, symbolizing her, go away. Evidence for Freud in favour of this interpretation included his observation that, a year later, when Ernst was presumably two and a half years old,

> [He] used to take a toy, if he was angry with it, and throw it on the floor, exclaiming: 'Go to the fwont!' He had heard at that time that his absent father was 'at the front' [in the 1914–1918 World War], and was far from regretting his absence; on the contrary he made it quite clear that he had no desire to be disturbed in his sole possession of his mother. (Freud, 1920a, p. 16)

This fitted in with Freud's previously formulated account of four-year-old Hans's Oedipal wish that his father would be absent so he, Hans, could have his mother to himself (see pp. 65–68 above).

Following the end of the 1914–1918 World War, Freud not only revised his previous wish-fulfilling theory of dreams with his death instinct-based theory of repeated nightmares and trauma. He also revised his theory of the Oedipus complex by linking it with what he described as the boy's castration complex and the girl's penis envy.

Due to the infant's initial bisexuality – their entertaining both active and passive, masculine and feminine wishes or desire – the 'complete Oedipus complex', said Freud, involves desire for the opposite sex parent and rivalry with the same sex parent as well as desire for the same sex parent and rivalry with the opposite sex parent (Freud, 1923a, p. 33). Or as Freud put it in the case of the boy,

> He could put himself in his father's place in a masculine fashion and have intercourse with his mother as his father did, in which case he would soon have felt the latter as a hindrance; or he might want to take the place of his mother and be loved by his father, in which case his mother would become superfluous. (Freud, 1923b, p. 176)

To this Freud added that the trauma of the boy's castration complex brings his masculine or heterosexual *and* his feminine or homosexual Oedipus complex to an end since, said Freud,

> both of them entailed the loss of his penis – the masculine one as a resulting punishment and the feminine one as a precondition. (Freud, 1923b, p. 176)

Drawing on his previously developed account of identification as defence against loss in melancholia or severe depression (Freud, 1917, p. 249), and on his account of men identifying with the leader of the army or church as an 'ego ideal' (Freud, 1921, p.129), Freud argued that the boy, faced with the trauma of castration, abandons his heterosexual or homosexual Oedipus complex. He does this by identifying with, or introjecting his father or both his parents into his ego where they become the nucleus of his superego representing 'prohibition against incest' (Freud, 1923b, p. 177).

What, though, of the girl's Oedipus and castration complexes? In her case, argued Freud, the castration complex, or trauma of castration, precedes her Oedipus complex desire for her father in competition with her mother. Her castration complex consists in penis envy, of which Freud claimed,

> [Girls] notice the penis of a brother or playmate, strikingly visible and of large proportions, at once recognize it as the superior counterpart of their own small and inconspicuous organ, and from that time forward fall a victim to envy for the penis. (Freud, 1925b, p. 252)

Freud argued that defences against this trauma include 'masculinity complex [...] hope of some day obtaining a penis' or the girl behaving 'as though she were a man'. They might involve her developing 'a sense of inferiority', 'jealousy', blaming her mother for her 'lack of a penis', or her rejection of clitoridal masturbation as 'a masculine activity' (Freud, 1925b, pp. 253, 254, 255).

This last response, said Freud, makes room for the girl's 'development of her femininity' (Freud, 1925b, p. 255):

> She gives up her wish for a penis and puts in place of it a wish for a child: and *with that purpose in view* she takes her father as a love-object. Her mother becomes the object of her jealousy. (Freud, 1925b, p. 256, italics in original)

Thus, whereas the boy's castration anxiety or trauma ends his Oedipus complex, the girl's castration trauma — her penis envy — brings her Oedipus complex into existence. It therefore cannot end it as it does in the boy, thereby inaugurating, according to Freud, his superego identification with his father's or both his parents' prohibition of incest and their superego more generally. As a result, argued Freud,

> [Women's] super-ego is never so inexorable, so impersonal, so independent of its emotional origins as we require it to be in men. Character-traits which critics of every epoch have brought up against women – that they show less sense of justice than men, that they are less ready to submit to the great exigencies of life, that they are more often influenced in their judgements by feelings of affection or hostility – all these would be amply accounted for by the modification in the formation of their super-ego which we have inferred above. (Freud, 1925b, pp. 257–258)

Not surprisingly, together with Freud's penis envy theory of women's psychology, his account of their relative lack of superego has caused considerable feminist furore (as I detail on pp. 181–183 below).

SUMMARY: In the mid-1920s, Freud theorized the Oedipus complex as brought to an end in the boy by the castration complex, and as initiated in the girl by her reaction to the female form of the castration complex constituted by what he controversially described as penis envy.

ID-EGO-SUPEREGO

Freud's 1923 account of the Oedipus complex, castration, and penis envy went along with his developing an id-ego-superego model of the mind. It was based in part on the concept of the 'It' developed by Georg Groddeck, a doctor sympathetic to psychoanalysis who used this concept to designate 'unknown and uncontrollable forces' by which we are 'lived'. Freud renamed these forces the 'id'. He described the 'id' as acting 'as though it were *Ucs* [unconscious]' (Freud, 1923a, p. 23).

Unlike Groddeck, who regarded the 'It' as regulating everything we do, Freud described the 'id' as regulated by the ego, of which he famously said,

> [I]n its relation to the id it is like a man on horseback, who has to hold in check the superior strength of the horse; with this difference, that the rider tries to do so with his own strength while the ego uses borrowed forces. The analogy may be carried a little further. Often a rider, if he is not to be parted from his horse, is obliged to guide it where it wants to go; so in the same way the ego is in the habit of transforming the id's will into action as if it were its own. (Freud, 1923a, p. 25)

Previously Freud had implied that the ego was equivalent to the conscious mind. By 1923, however, he was convinced that, since resistance to becoming conscious of what is repressed and unconscious emanates from the ego, it too must be partly unconscious.

How, though, does what is unconscious become conscious? It only does so, according to Freud, through sensations and feelings reaching the preconscious system of the mind. Examples of this unconscious-to-preconscious process included for him 'word-presentations' whereby, he said, 'internal thought-processes are made into perceptions' – a process which is, of course, crucial to talking cure psychoanalytic treatment (Freud, 1923a, p. 23).

To this Freud added an account of the ego based on his previously developed theory that those who are severely depressed and melancholic defensively identify in their ego with those they have loved, hated, and lost (see p. 130 above). Now in his 1923 book, *The Ego and the Id*, he argued that the ego in all of us is the product of identification with those whom we cathect or invest with feeling – our parents, for instance – from whom we grow away. He accordingly claimed that 'the ego is a precipitate of abandoned object-cathexes' (Freud, 1923a, p. 29).

The superego, he maintained, results from another aspect of child development, namely the Oedipus and castration complex. In defending against this complex, he argued, the child identifies with the father as a superego figure in its mind representing society's taboo on incest. Writing more about this outcome of the Oedipus and castration complex, he explained,

> The child's parents, and especially [the child's] father, were perceived as the obstacle to a realization of his Oedipus wishes; so his infantile ego fortified itself for the carrying out of the repression by erecting this same obstacle within itself. It borrowed strength to do this [...] from the father [...] The super-ego retains the character of the father, while the more powerful the Oedipus complex was and the more rapidly it succumbed to repression (under the influence of authority, religious teaching, schooling and reading), the stricter will be the domination of the super-ego over the ego later on – in the form of conscience or perhaps of an unconscious sense of guilt. (Freud, 1923a, pp. 34–35)

This unconscious sense of guilt, Freud added, is responsible for the 'negative therapeutic reaction' whereby patients in psychoanalysis cling to their psychological ills as a form of self-punishment (Freud, 1923a, pp. 37, 49).

Expanding on this issue, the psychoanalyst Joan Riviere (1936), the translator from German into English of Freud's 1923 book, *The Ego and the Id*, attributed the negative therapeutic reaction to the patient's control, contempt, and denial of any value in what the psychoanalyst says or does. It serves, she said, as an organized mask or defence against the patient's inward experience of those with whom they are most involved. Since this mask is an organized defence, piecemeal interpretation is of little use because, in this state of mind, the patient is determined to maintain the status quo. They refuse to change. They reject any improvement or praise just as, in her psychoanalytic treatment by Freud, Riviere rejected praise from him.

Meanwhile, Freud had redescribed psychological ills in id-ego-superego terms. He described symptoms of hysteria and other '[t]ransference neuroses' as involving conflict between the ego and the id; 'narcissistic neuroses', such as melancholia, as involving conflict between the ego and the superego; and delusions in 'psychoses' as involving conflict between the 'ego' and 'the external world' (Freud, 1924, p. 152).

To this Freud (1926) added a new account of psychological ills. He attributed them to anxiety or fear of danger from the external world, from something repressed and unconscious, or from fear of the superego as a more or less ill-defined monstrous figure within the mind.

Freud accordingly redefined the goal of psychoanalytic treatment. Previously he had described its aim, at least as regards neurosis, as that of enabling patients to become conscious of the repressed and unconscious cause of their neurotic ills. In his 1933 *New Introductory Lectures on Psycho-Analysis*, however, he said of the goal of psychoanalytic treatment,

> Its intention is, indeed, to strengthen the ego, to make it more independent of the super-ego, to widen its field of perception and enlarge its organization, so that it can appropriate fresh portions of the id. Where id was, there ego shall be. It is a work of culture – not unlike the draining of the Zuider Zee. (Freud, 1933a, p. 80)

It was a goal his psychoanalyst daughter, Anna Freud, reiterated in her 1936 book, *The Ego and the Mechanisms of Defence*, a copy of which she gave Freud in honour of his eightieth birthday that May. She concluded this book by insisting that the aim of psychoanalytic treatment is to secure victory of the patient's 'ego' through establishing 'the most harmonious relations possible between the id, the superego, and the forces of the outside world' (A. Freud, 1936, p. 176).

This version of psychoanalysis was developed by the psychoanalysts Heinz Hartmann, Ernst Kris, and Rudolph Lowenstein after they fled fascist and anti-Semitic Europe in the 1930s for the United States. Here they developed what became known as ego psychology. This included emphasis by Hartmann (1939, 1964) on the innate capacity of the ego to facilitate the adaptation of individuals to the environment in which they live. This version of psychoanalysis was in turn developed by the psychoanalyst Heinz Kohut (1971). He recommended psychoanalysts to strengthen the patient's ego by facilitating their development of a mirroring and idealizing transference experience of them.

The psychoanalyst Jacques Lacan, who had been psychoanalysed by Rudolph Lowenstein, was appalled. He insisted that the ego is an illusion rooted in the six- to eighteen-month-old infant misidentifying itself with the unitary image it sees of itself in the mirror. Describing this process, Lacan observed,

> Unable as yet to walk, or even to stand up, and held tightly as he is by some support, human or artificial (what, in France, we call a '*trotte-bébé*'), he [the infant] nevertheless overcomes, in a flutter of jubilant activity, the obstructions of his support and, fixing his attitude in a slightly leaning-forward position, in order to hold it in his gaze, brings back an instantaneous aspect of the image. [...] This jubilant assumption of his specular [mirror] image by the child at the *infans* stage, still sunk in his motor incapacity and nursling dependence, would seem to exhibit in an exemplary situation the symbolic matrix in which the *I* [ego] is precipitated in a primordial form, before it is objectified in the dialectic of identification with the other, and before language restores to it, in the universal, its function as subject. (Lacan, 1949, pp. 1–2, italics in original)

Lacan called this mirror stage an aspect of the imaginary. In doing so he replaced Freud's id-ego-superego model of the mind with a real-imaginary-symbolic model.

Appalled by ego psychology, Lacan was much more in favour of what has been described as the object relations theory version of psychoanalysis developed by, among others, the psychoanalyst Melanie Klein. Building on Freud's theory of the superego, Klein characterized the inner world of infants, children, and adults as furnished with object relations representations of their relations with others.

Examples for Klein (1945) included a ten-year-old patient, Richard, who she argued represented his relations with his mother, father, brother, and himself by, respectively, light blue, black, purple, and red shapes in drawings inspired by a map of the British Empire in the room in which his psychoanalytic treatment by Klein took place. Applauding such drawings (two of which are illustrated here), Lacan argued,

> Through [Klein] we know the function of the imaginary primordial enclosure formed by the *imago* of the mother's body; through her we have the cartography, drawn by the children's own hands, of the mother's internal empire, the historical atlas of the intestinal divisions in which the *imagos* of the father and brothers (real or virtual), in which the voracious aggression of the subject himself, dispute their deleterious dominance over her sacred regions. We know, too, the persistence in the subject of this shadow of the *bad internal objects* [...] Klein pushes back the limits within which we can see the subjective function of identification operate, and in particular enables us to situate as perfectly original the first formation of the superego.
> (Lacan, 1948, pp. 20–21)

This is not easy to understand. Nevertheless, subsequent object relations theory (ORT) developments of the work of Klein and other psychoanalysts inform a great deal of psychoanalytic treatment today. This has resulted in less reference by psychoanalysts to what is repressed and unconscious in the patient's mind and in much more reference to their inner world.

ID-EGO-SUPEREGO 147

BLACK
LIGHT BLUE
PURPLE
RED

Figure 24.1 Two of Richard's empire drawings
Courtesy Melanie Klein Trust

Recent examples include the account by a psychoanalytic psychotherapist, Jonathan Radcliffe, of his treatment of a forty-five-year-old woman, Frances. Her psychological problems included depression, occasional rages, self-hatred, envy, and sadness following the end of her marriage some years before.

In explaining his ORT approach to her treatment, Radcliffe recalls as follows conversations between himself and Frances regarding her involvement in a garden scheme:

> On her first day [in this scheme], an older woman, who Frances perceived as intimidating, criticized her. Frances said this made her want to leave and not go back. [...] In our [treatment] session, [she] wept, saying that she had been stupid. I asked how she felt towards the woman. She said angry although she did not look it. Instead, she criticized herself for being useless, before saying, helplessly, 'What shall I do when I go back?' When I asked what she thought she should do, she said her inclination was to ignore this woman. I said that sounded like giving her the cold shoulder because she was angry. She admitted that was possible. She began the next session by confessing to not having gone back [to the garden scheme] so as not to have to face 'that woman'. She said she felt terrible that she was so immature compared to the others there, especially younger ones. I said perhaps she had not developed as she could have done, because of her life experiences. Frances became emotional, expressing shame and resentment at her immaturity. When I said this must be difficult she became tearful and started looking away. I felt she was removing herself from our relationship in that moment, so asked 'how are you feeling towards me right now?' She said that I thought she was no good and probably wanted her to leave because she was so useless. When pressed on the feeling towards me, she said she would like to shake me, knitting her hands together and clenching her fists. (Radcliffe & Yeomans, 2019, pp. 13–14)

Interpreting this in ORT terms, Radcliffe described Frances's inner world as peopled by aggressive object relations figures based perhaps on her experience of the relation between herself and her parents as a child. It seemed to him that she split off and projected an aggressive version of these object relation figures onto the woman in the garden scheme. Hence, he said, her fear of, followed by anger with, this woman. It also caused Frances to experience him, he argued, first as empathic and then as critical and dismissive. It was in these terms that he interpreted to Frances her experience sometimes as victim and sometimes as aggressor in her relationships with other people.

> *SUMMARY:* With his id-ego-superego model of the mind, Freud redescribed psychological ills and their treatment in terms of strengthening the patient's ego relative to their id and superego. The ego psychology version of psychoanalysis developed from this model has subsequently been variously modified and criticized. Others prefer the object relations theory version of psychoanalysis to which Freud's attention to the superego has given rise.

CONCLUSIONS TO PART V

During and after the 1914–1918 World War, Freud transformed psychoanalysis. This included his attributing severe depression or melancholia to defensive identification with those who have been loved, hated, and lost. It also included his developing a death instinct based theory of the repetition of trauma, and his describing the Oedipus complex in terms of the more or less traumatic effect of castration anxiety in boys and penis envy in girls. This was related to his forging an id-ego-superego structural model of the mind subsequently developed by him and his followers into what has become known as ego psychology, and by the psychoanalyst Melanie Klein and others into an objects relations theory version of psychoanalysis which is still widely used within and beyond psychoanalytically informed clinical practice today.

PART VI
BEYOND CLINICAL PSYCHOANALYSIS

Also still very influential today is Freud's extension of psychoanalysis beyond its clinical practice. This includes its influence on biographical writing and on the content and psychological impact of art, drama, and film. This is due not least to his psychoanalytic biographies of Leonardo da Vinci and Fyodor Dostoevsky; his psychoanalytic account of, for instance, the content of Shakespeare's *Hamlet* and Ibsen's *Rosmersholm*; and his psychoanalytic interpretation of the impact of, for example, Sophocles's *Oedipus Rex* and Michelangelo's sculpture *Moses*. This chapter ends with sections highlighting the extension of psychoanalysis by Freud and his followers to anthropology, religion, sociology, gender politics, and racism, of which he was a victim when together with his family he had to flee anti-Semitic, Germany-invaded Vienna for London, where, having been ill for many years with cancer, he died aged eighty-three on 23 September 1939.

ART, LITERATURE, FILM

For someone like Freud, very much involved with the art world of his time, it is perhaps no surprise that he extended psychoanalysis beyond its clinical practice in writing about artists and writers, the content of their work, and its impact. Nor is it any surprise that, influenced by Freud, others have used his psychoanalytic ideas in creating, thinking, and writing about art, literature, and film.

ARTISTS AND WRITERS

In applying his clinically based psychoanalytic ideas to artists and creative writers, Freud (e.g. 1908a) emphasized the fantasy-based inspiration of their work. He also wrote about art involving the sublimation by its creators of their sexual instinct or drive in pursuit of 'higher aims' than sex (Freud, 1908b, p. 161).

It was in terms of fantasy and sublimation that he wrote his first and only book-length biography – a case study of the artist Leonardo da Vinci. In doing so he noted that Leonardo connected his achievement – specifically research into the flight of birds – to a fantasy of which, according to Freud, he said,

> I recall as one of my very earliest memories that while I was in my cradle a vulture came down to me, and opened my mouth with its tail, and struck me many times with its tail against my lips. (Freud, 1910b, p. 82)

Freud psychoanalysed this fantasy as the product of Leonardo's wish-fulfilling pleasure as a baby sucking at his mother's breast – a psychoanalytic interpretation Freud based on the speculation that, for Leonardo, the vulture's tail served as a symbol of the penis.

Why a penis? Because, Freud speculated, Leonardo narcissistically adopted others who like him had a penis as object of his sexual desire. Hence his homosexuality. It enabled him, claimed Freud, to preserve repressed and unconscious desire for his mother, to whom he remained faithful by sexually pursuing boys and men, not girls and women like her.

From Leonardo's scientific interest in, and fantasy about a vulture – more accurately a kite, not a vulture – Freud turned to Leonardo's well-known portrait *Mona Lisa*. Previously, the British art critic Walter Pater (1873) had speculated that on first meeting the subject of this portrait her face reminded Leonardo of a wishful fantasy of an 'ideal lady' emerging from 'the fabric of his dreams'. Quoting Pater approvingly, Freud claimed that Mona Lisa's face evoked a memory in Leonardo of 'the smile of bliss and rapture which had once played on his mother's lips as she fondled him' (Freud, 1910b, pp. 110, 117).

Previously, Freud speculated, Leonardo had repressed this memory and forbidden himself 'to desire such caresses from the lips of women' (Freud, 1910b, p. 117). Seeing Mona Lisa's face broke through this repression. It evoked, Freud claimed, a wish-fulfilling fantasy or memory in Leonardo of his mother, Caterina, or of his stepmother, Donna Albiera, smiling at him when he was a young child.

Hence, Freud maintained, the mysterious smile given by Leonardo to Mona Lisa in his portrait of her; the mysterious smile given by him to the Madonna and St Anne as young women gazing beatifically on the infant Jesus in his painting *Madonna and Child with St. Anne*; and the same smile playing on the lips of the man pictured in Leonardo's painting *Saint John the Baptist*. Unfortunately for this theory, however,

Leonardo had already given the Madonna and St Anne this mysterious smile in a drawing entitled *The Virgin and Child with St. Anne and the Infant John the Baptist*, which he completed before he ever met Mona Lisa.

This undermines the credibility of Freud's psychoanalytic account of Leonardo's work as an artist. It might also be objected that psychoanalytic biography of great people serves no useful purpose. Such objections result, Freud argued, from the wish to idealize them. Much better to psychoanalyse the great – warts and all – rather than indulge in hagiography, he maintained, in justifying psychoanalytic biography. Yet he concluded his biography of Leonardo by idealizing him, specifically his 'extraordinary capacity for sublimating the primitive instincts' (Freud, 1910b, p. 136).

Not only is sublimation crucial to the work of the artist. Also crucial, Freud maintained, is the artist's inspiration by fantasy. So saying, and generalizing his account of the fantasy-based inspiration of Leonardo's art, Freud argued,

> An artist is originally a man who turns away from reality because he cannot come to terms with the renunciation of instinctual satisfaction which it at first demands, and who allows his erotic and ambitious wishes full play in the life of phantasy. He finds the way back to reality, however, from this world of phantasy by making use of special gifts to mould his phantasies into truths of a new kind, which are valued by men as precious reflections of reality. (Freud, 1911a, p. 224)

The art historian Ernst Gombrich (1954) was appalled by the priority Freud gave to fantasy as inspiration for art. In doing so, said Gombrich, Freud and his followers wrongly assimilated art to his psychoanalytic theory of dreams and thereby ignored ways in which historical factors shape the artist's work. Certainly this was true of surrealist artists insofar as, inspired by Freud, they looked to dreams and fantasy as inspiration of their work.

In doing so they overlooked Freud's observation that, whatever their inwardly determined content, dreams are also often provoked by external stimuli (see p. 32 above). This was particularly brought home to me by reading the psychoanalytically minded artist and psychotherapist Patricia Townsend's 2019 published psychoanalytic book, *Creative States of Mind*.

Long before this book's publication, and despite his psychoanalytic biography of Leonardo not being well received, Freud wrote another psychoanalytic biography, not of Leonardo da Vinci but of the novelist Fyodor Dostoevsky. In doing so Freud drew on his psychoanalytic theory that boys resolve conflict between love and hate of their father by identifying with him, this forming the basis of their superego-caused 'sense of guilt' (Freud, 1928, p. 183).

Because his father was particularly violent, Freud argued, Dostoevsky suffered more than most from wanting to kill his father and from superego-caused feelings of guilt. These feelings, Freud claimed, were a cause of Dostoevesky's epilepsy and of his self-punishing addiction to gambling. They also contributed, Freud maintained, to Dostoevsky's depiction of father-murder in his novel *The Brothers Karamazov*, which Freud praised as 'the most magnificent novel ever written' (Freud, 1928, p. 177).

This and other writings by Freud have had a major influence on subsequent biographical writing. They include the psychoanalyst Hanna Segal's argument that art only has aesthetic value provided its creator seeks, with it, to repair the ill-effects of destructive impulses within themselves. It was in these terms that Segal (1952, 1984) wrote biographically about Marcel Proust, Joseph Conrad, and their novels. Other Freud-inspired or at least quasi-psychoanalytic biographies of creative artists include Bernardo Bertolucci's (e.g. 2001) account of his life and work as a film director, and William Feaver's (2019) account of the life of Freud's artist grandson Lucian Freud.

ART'S CONTENT

As well as using psychoanalysis in writing biographically about artists and creative writers, Freud also psychoanalysed the content of art. Its content or 'subject-matter' was, he admitted the aspect of art which most attracted him to it (Freud, 1914d, p. 211).

It was the content of Sophocles's play *Oedipus Rex*, depicting Oedipus murdering his father and marrying his mother, that attracted Freud to refer to this work of art in supporting his psychoanalytic claim regarding the universality of the infant's jealousy of the father for love of the mother. He was also attracted to the content of William Shakespeare's play *Hamlet*, depicting Hamlet's resistance to avenging his father's murder by his stepfather, Claudius, resistance which Freud attributed to Hamlet having 'meditated' doing the same deed as Claudius due to passion for Hamlet's mother, Gertrude (Freud, 1897, p. 266).

It was likewise the content of a novella, *Gradiva*, depicting a young man's obsession with a sculpture prompting a dream and the revival of a previously repressed desire for a childhood friend, that inspired Freud (1907a) to write psychoanalytically about this novella. Freud (1914d) was also fascinated by the content of Michelangelo's sculpture *Moses*, specifically its depiction of Moses after he had received the Ten Commandments from God.

Freud (1916) went on to use the content of Shakespeare's play *Macbeth* and Henrik Ibsen's play *Rosmersholm* to illustrate ways in which guilt can ruin success. Freud (1928) later illustrated his questionable theory that young men desire to have sex with their mothers to save them from masturbation with the story told by his friend the novelist Stefan Zweig in a novella, *Twenty-Four Hours in the Life of a Woman*.

The psychoanalytic ideas of Freud have in turn informed the content of many examples of art, drama, fiction, and film. Examples include Italo Svevo's 1923 novel *Confessions of Zeno*; Salvador Dali's painting *Metamorphosis of Narcissus*, which Dali showed Freud when they met in 1937; as well as many films including Orson Welles's 1941 film *Citizen Kane*, Alfred Hitchcock's 1958 film *Vertigo*, and Nanni Moretti's 2011 film *We Have a Pope*.

Psychoanalysts also feature in films. Examples include the 1999–2007 TV series *The Sopranos*, and David Conrenberg's 2011 film *A Dangerous Method*, featuring Freud, Jung, and Jung's psychoanalytic patient Sabina Spielrein.

ART'S IMPACT

Not only did Freud use psychoanalysis in his account of artists, creative writers, and the content of their work. He also discussed psychoanalytically the impact of works of art. Examples include his saying of the impact of Sophocles's above-mentioned drama *Oedipus Rex*,

> Each member of the audience was once, in germ and in phantasy, just such an Oedipus, and each one recoils in horror from the dream-fulfilment here transplanted into reality, with the whole quota of repression which separates his infantile state from his present one. (Freud, 1897, p. 265)

Writing more generally about the impact on him of works of art, Freud observed,

> [W]orks of art do exercise a powerful effect on me, especially those of literature and sculpture, less often of painting. This has occasioned me, when I have been contemplating such things, to spend a long time before them trying to apprehend them in my own way, i.e. to explain to myself what their effect is due to. Whenever I cannot do this, as for instance with music, I am almost incapable of obtaining any pleasure. (Freud, 1914d, p. 211)

Freud might not have been keen on music. But he was keen on Michelangelo's above-mentioned sculpture, *Moses*. To explain its powerful impact on him, Freud sought to discover Michelangelo's motive in creating it. Free associating to details of this sculpture, he arrived at the speculation that, in creating it, Michelangelo sought 'to make the passage of a violent gust of passion visible in the signs left behind it in the ensuing calm' (Freud, 1914d, p. 236).

Others, influenced by Freud, have focused more on the impact on artists and their public of the physical stuff of art. Criticizing artists who imposed their fantasy on the physical stuff or material of their art in creating it, the psychoanalytically minded art critic Adrian Stokes (1934) applauded, by contrast, artists who responded to this material by giving form, in their art, to the fantasies it evokes.

The psychoanalyst Marion Milner (1950) likewise attended to the physical material of her doodle drawings and to the fantasies it evoked. So did her close friend, the psychoanalyst Donald Winnicott (1953), in playing the squiggle game with his child patients, a game in which players take turns to make a doodle for the other player to complete into a picture. In using this game in psychoanalytic work with his child patients, Winnicott paid attention to the impact of the resulting squiggle pictures on his child patients in evoking memories and fantasies relevant to understanding their psychological problems – an issue also explored in today's art therapy, whether or not it is psychoanalytically informed.

A rather different tack involving art and psychoanalysis was developed by the psychoanalyst Wilfred Bion. He likened the impact of painting to that of the impact of a psychoanalyst's interpretation on his or her patient. With this together with Freud's concept of the dream-work transformation of unconscious wishes into consciously recalled dreams, Bion used the term dream-work-α to designate the means by which the artist transforms his or her sense-data experience into a work of art. Bion said of this process of transformation,

> [The artist] is someone who is able to digest facts, i.e. sense data, and then to present the digested facts, my α-elements, in a way that makes it possible for the weak assimilators to go on from there. Thus the artist [Vermeer] helps the non-artist to digest, say, the Little Street in Delft by doing α-work on his sense impressions and 'publishing' the result so that others who could not 'dream' the Little Street itself can now digest the published α-work of someone who could digest it. (Bion, 1960, pp. 143–144)

Bion (1965) went on to liken the impact on the psychoanalytic patient of a psychoanalyst's interpretation, based on the psychoanalyst transforming their impressions of what goes on in the patient's psychoanalytic treatment, to the impact on the beholder of Claude Monet's transformation of his impressions of a poppy field into his painting *Poppies*. This in turn influences the account by the psychoanalysts John Schneider (2010), Howard Levine (2012), and others of ways psychoanalysis can be helpful to patients today.

Psychoanalytically minded writers have also attended to the psychological impact not only of visual art but also of movies on their beholders. They have described, for example, the voyeuristic impact on the moviegoer of the film *Peeping Tom* and the impact of the movies more generally in evoking the moviegoer's identification with the movie's central character or characters, an approach which has been criticized for its male-centredness by the psychoanalytically minded film theorist Laura Mulvey (1975).

More recently psychoanalytically minded writers have paid attention to the physical processes including camerawork involved in film-making. Nevertheless, as the psychoanalyst Andrea Sabbadini points out regarding the impact of film on the moviegoer,

> [W]hile always potentially aware of the existence of a camera somewhere in the background of their viewing experience, [moviegoers] grow out of it once they feel settled in their armchairs (sometimes with the help of a drink and a tub of popcorn) and the light in the cinema goes down. They can then immerse themselves in the film's narrative, feel held and contained by it, and let themselves be drawn into a complex play of identifications with, and relationships to, the different characters on the screen. (Sabbadini, 2016, p. 343)

This is arguably in keeping with the perspective of Susan Sontag (1966). Rejecting interpretative approaches, like those of Freud, in writing about the content of art, she urged her readers to pay attention to its sensory impact. She urged them to see, hear, and feel more.

In keeping with this approach is the work of the psychoanalyst Julia Kristeva (1980). Drawing on Freud's (1923a) account of the unconscious becoming conscious through its perceptual residues (see p. 143 above), she highlights the sensory impact on its beholders of the colour of Giotto's fresco paintings in the Arena Chapel in Padua (Kristeva, 1980, p. 217).

She has also famously drawn attention to the impact of the 'semiotic' stuff of poetry on its listeners (Kristeva, 1984, p. 43). The literary

critic Ruth Felski likewise emphasizes the importan
attention to the sensory impact of literature rather th
psychoanalytically in terms of 'symptoms, repressions,
vowels, rifts, cracks and fissures' (Eagleton, 2017, p. 35).

> *SUMMARY:* Freud extended psychoanalysis to his account of artists and writers, and to his account of the content and impact of art. So too have his followers in writing psychoanalytic biographies of artists, writers, and others, and in writing psychoanalytically about the content and impact of art, literature, and film.

ANTHROPOLOGY

As well as using clinical findings from psychoanalysis in writing about artists and writers, and about the content and impact of their work, Freud also used his clinical findings in writing about anthropology. Together with Jung in the early days of psychoanalysis, Freud was inspired by anthropological findings reported in the 1905 book *The Secret of the Totem*, by Andrew Lang, and in the four-volume 1910 book *Totemism and Exogamy*, by J. G. Frazer. Drawing on these and other anthropological works, Freud wrote a book, *Totem and Taboo*, consisting of articles first published in his and his psychoanalyst colleagues', Otto Rank's and Hanns Sachs's, journal *Imago*, specializing in non-clinical applications of psychoanalysis.

The book itself begins with anthropological data from Australia about clan societies, each of which, as described by Frazer, took as its totem an animal to represent the clan's tribal ancestor. Since all members of the clan were descended from the same tribal ancestor, they were not allowed to have sexual relations with each other. Hence the 'horror of incest' in such societies (Freud, 1913b, p.1).

From this horror and the incest taboo which it involves, Freud turned to taboo prohibitions more generally. They are all means of warding off demonic power, he maintained. He likened them to the prohibitions involved in obsessive compulsive disorder (OCD). Examples included his patient Ernst Lanzer prohibiting himself from paying a debt on the orders of an army captain lest it result in Lanzer's father becoming the victim of a horrendous rat punishment (see p. 72 above).

Generalizing from patients like Lanzer, Freud argued that the self-imposed prohibitions of the OCD patient originate in early childhood experiences which they repress and displace onto their obsessions. These experiences, said Freud, involve hatred of, and wish to harm the father, a wish that is repressed and unconscious such that the patient is only consciously aware of their love for, and wish to protect their father. On this basis Freud argued that in all societies fear of violating taboo prohibitions is fuelled by the strength of the repressed and unconscious wish to do whatever the taboo forbids.

He also noted anthropological evidence that in some societies contact with their rulers is taboo. He related this to the belief in these societies that the ruler is a source of danger and also has to be protected. He linked this in turn with his horse-phobic patient, four-year-old Hans's fear of his father and worry lest he fall down and die (see p. 66 above).

Hans was evidently divided between hatred and love of his father. Similar hate-love ambivalence, argued Freud, causes the dead to be taboo. He related this to the observation that, as he put it,

> When a wife has lost her husband or a daughter her mother, it not infrequently happens that the survivor is overwhelmed by tormenting doubts [...] as to whether she may not herself have been responsible for the death of this cherished being through some act of carelessness or neglect. No amount of recollection of the care she lavished on the sufferer, no amount of objective disproof of the accusation, serves to bring the torment to an end. [...] We find that in a certain sense these obsessive self-reproaches are justified [...] It is not that the mourner was really responsible for the death or was really guilty of neglect [...] None the less there was something in her – a wish that was unconscious to herself – which would not have been dissatisfied by the occurrence of death and which might actually have brought it about if it had had the power. (Freud, 1913b, p. 60)

Freud accordingly concluded that it is fear of the dead retaliating against unconscious wishes that they die in those who cared for them when they were alive that makes the dead taboo.

The revelation by psychoanalysis that pathological mourning involves repressed and unconscious hatred of the dead contributed to Freud also suggesting that projection of this hatred onto the dead might account for the belief that 'souls of those who have just died are transformed into demons' (Freud, 1913b, p. 60). This adds to the dead being taboo, as is touching the dead, lest they return as hostile demons or ghosts – a taboo to which Freud (1919) returned in an essay about what is unsettling and uncanny.

He had meanwhile investigated anthropological observations regarding magical practices, such as rituals aimed at making it rain. To this he added the belief in some societies that knowing someone's name is a means of exercising power over them. He related this to one of his psychoanalytic patients, coining the phrase 'omnipotence of thoughts'. The patient gave the following examples:

> If he thought of someone, he would be sure to meet that very person immediately afterwards, as though by magic. If he suddenly asked after the health of an acquaintance whom he had not seen for a long time, he would hear that he had just died, so that it would look as though a telepathic message had arrived from him. If, without any really serious intention, he swore at some stranger, he might be sure that the man would die soon afterwards, so that he would feel responsible for his death. (Freud, 1913b, pp. 85, 86)

Freud also noted the omnipotent belief of children that, through magic, their wishes will be fulfilled.

From magic he returned to anthropological data about clan societies and their taboo on members of the same clan having sex with each other because as descendants of the same ancestral father, represented by the clan's totem animal, this constituted incest. Freud related this taboo to four-year-old Hans displacing fear of his father in competition with him for his mother onto fear of horses. Just as horses thereby became a substitute for Hans's father, said Freud, the clan's totem animal becomes a substitute for the clan's ancestral father.

Why, then, the sacramental killing and communal eating of the totem animal in clan societies given that killing and eating the clan's totem is also taboo in these societies? In answering this question, Freud drew on the evolutionary biologist Charles Darwin's deduction, based on non-human primate data, that as Darwin put it,

> [P]rimaeval man aboriginally lived in small communities, each with as many wives as he could support and obtain, whom he would have jealously guarded against all other men. Or he may have lived with several wives by himself, like the Gorilla [...] [so that] when the young male grows up, a contest takes place for mastery, and the strongest, by killing and driving out the others, establishes himself as the head of the community. (in Freud, 1913b, p. 125)

Armed with this deduction, together with evidence of the ritual killing and communal eating of the totem animal in clan societies, Freud speculated that an occasion occurred in what Darwin described as the 'primal horde' of human prehistory when

> [B]rothers who had been driven out came together, killed and devoured their father and so made an end to the patriarchal horde [...] [Subsequently a] sense of guilt made its appearance [...] What had up to then been prevented by [the father's] actual existence was thenceforward prohibited by the sons themselves [...] They revoked their deed by forbidding the killing of the totem, the substitute for their father; and they renounced its fruits by resigning their claim to the women who had now been set free. (Freud, 1913b, p. 143)

Herein, argued Freud, resides the origin of the taboo on father-murder and on incest with the mother. This corresponds to what, on the basis of his psychoanalytic work, he described as 'the two repressed wishes of the Oedipus complex' (Freud, 1913b, p. 143). He went on to relate the sacramental killing and communal eating of the totem animal in clan societies to the Christian ritual of Holy Communion, in which the flesh and blood of God's son, Jesus, is symbolically eaten and drunk in the form of bread and wine.

Following publication of his resulting book, *Totem and Taboo*, Freud (1918a) wrote more about anthropological data. They included evidence of a taboo on virginity expressed in rituals involving the rupture of the girl's hymen when she reaches puberty or prior to her wedding night. He also noted anthropological evidence indicating a taboo not only on virginity but also on women's menstruation, pregnancy, and childbirth.

As with every other taboo, he argued, the taboo on virginity is a protection against danger. He psychoanalysed this danger as related to fear of woman lest, in her first experience of sexual intercourse, she give vent to 'unconcealed expression to her hostility towards the man by abusing him, raising her hand against him or actually striking him' (Freud, 1918a, p. 201).

Hence, Freud maintained, the following anthropologically observed custom in some societies whereby

> [A]fter the hymen has been ruptured (by hand or with some instrument) there follows a ceremonial act of coitus or mock-intercourse with the representatives of the husband, and this proves to us that the purpose of the taboo observance is not fulfilled by avoiding anatomical defloration, that the husband is to be spared something else as well as the woman's reaction to the painful injury. (Freud, 1918a, p. 202)

What are the men to be spared? The ravages of women's penis envy, said Freud. To this he added the following clinical evidence for women's supposed envy of the penis:

> We have learnt from the analysis of many neurotic women that they go through an early age in which they envy their brothers their sign of masculinity and feel at a disadvantage and humiliated because of the lack of it (actually because of its diminished size) in themselves. (Freud, 1918a, p. 204)

Having made this tendentious claim (about which more on pp. 181–183 below), Freud went on to describe a woman patient who had recently married having a dream which he interpreted as signifying her 'wish to castrate her young husband to keep his penis for herself' (Freud, 1918a, p. 206).

Despite this questionable interpretation Freud's work was very much appreciated by the leading anthropologist, Bronislaw Malinowski. Although he questioned Freud's claim regarding the universality of the Oedipus complex, Malinowski acknowledged, in a preface to his book, *Sex and Repression in Savage Society*, his debt as an anthropologist to Freud for his 'dynamic theory of mind', attention to child and developmental psychology, and to repressed unconscious 'unofficial and unacknowledged sides of life' (Malinowski, 1927, pp. vii).

Psychoanalysis compelled Malinowski 'to place the social force of repressed passions and longings at the center of [anthropological] attention', conclude today's anthropologists Tine Gammeltoft and Lotte Segal (2016, p. 400). Long before that, Karl Marx's close friend and collaborator, Friedrich Engels (1884), argued on the basis of anthropological data that societies were originally organized on a female-dominated matriarchal basis. By contrast, Freud (1913b) used anthropological data in asserting the male-dominated patriarchal organization of the various societies he described. So did the anthropologist Claude Lévi-Strauss (1949). He maintained that all societies are structurally patriarchal.

The psychoanalyst Jacques Lacan followed suit. In doing so he wrote approvingly about Freud's *Totem and Taboo* account of the father-centred origin of patriarchally organized clan societies. He also argued that, with his account of the genital or phallic stage of psychosexual development, Freud highlighted the way in which, through the Oedipus and the castration complex involving the antithesis of having a penis or being castrated, Freud indicated how children learn the meaning of the phallus, the central symbol of patriarchy, according to Lacan.

To this anthropologically based development of psychoanalysis the psychoanalyst and feminist Julia Kristeva (1982) added further reflections about Freud's *Totem and Taboo* account of the horror of incest. Unlike Freud, however, she put this in terms of horror of return to oneness with the mother and nature prior to entry, via the Oedipus and the castration complex, into patriarchally organized culture. It is this horror, she said, which accounts for the taboo not so much on women's sexuality but on what is related to mothering – specifically menstruation and childbirth.

Kristeva's resulting book, *Powers of Horror*, in which she describes women's mother-related biological functions as abject and taboo, has inspired what has been described as abject art. It has also inspired feminist writing, including Barbara Creed's cultural studies book, *The Monstrous-Feminine*, and its critique by the sociologist Imogen Tyler, author of *Revolting Subjects*. In this and other ways Freud's extension of psychoanalysis to the social sciences, specifically anthropology with his book *Totem and Taboo*, continues in psychoanalysis and beyond today.

> *SUMMARY:* With his book *Totem and Taboo*, Freud used findings from his clinical work as a psychoanalyst to explain anthropological data regarding various taboo practices some of which he related to the murder of the patriarchal leader of the primal horde. This in turn was used by the psychoanalyst Jacques Lacan in recasting Freud's theory of the Oedipus and the castration complex in patriarchal terms, to which feminists and others have added in recent years.

RELIGION

Religion figured a great deal in Freud's life. He was brought up in the Jewish religion. So was his father, Jacob. Although Jacob eventually dispensed with all religious observances, except Purim and Passover, he continued to read the Talmud and Torah in the holy language, Hebrew. And this very much influenced Freud.

Evidence of this comes from Freud's biographer, Ernest Jones. He reports that, in a copy of the Bible given to him by Jacob, Freud wrote,

> It was in the seventh year of your age that the spirit of God began to move you to learning. I would say the spirit of God speaketh to you: 'Read in My Book; there will be opened to thee sources of knowledge and of the intellect'. It is the Book of Books. (In Jones, 1961, p. 47)

'My deep engrossment in the Bible story (almost as soon as I had learnt the art of reading) had, as I recognized much later, an enduring effect upon the direction of my interest', Freud himself later recalled (Freud, 1925c, p. 8). At secondary school he had been taught Hebrew and the Jewish religion by Samuel Hammerschlag, after whose daughter, Anna, Freud named his youngest child.

Alongside studying anatomy, chemistry, and physiology at university, he studied philosophy with a priest, Franz Brentano. Telling his friend Eduard Silberstein, in November 1874, about his attendance at Brentano's classes, Freud said,

> I, the godless medical man and empiricist, am attending two courses in philosophy [...] One of the courses – listen and marvel! – deals with the existence of God. (In Boehlich, 1990, p. 70)

'For the time being', he wrote the following March 1875, 'I have ceased to be a materialist and am not yet a theist'. He was nevertheless bothered by Brentano's arguments persuading him that 'the science of all things seems to demand the existence of God' (in Boehlich, 1990, pp. 104–105, 111).

Opposed like his father, Jacob, to religious observances, Freud upset his wife, Martha, beginning on the very first Friday after their marriage in September 1886, with his refusal to let her perform the Jewish ritual of lighting the Sabbath lights that evening. He went on to psychoanalyze religious rituals in terms of their serving as means of repressing guilt-evoking sexual feelings.

He likened these rituals to the symptoms of obsessive compulsive disorder, of which he gave the following example of a patient of whom he said,

> [She] was under a compulsion to rinse round her washbasin several times after washing. The significance of this ceremonial action lay in the proverbial saying: 'Don't throw away dirty water till you have clean'. Her action was intended to give a warning to her sister, of whom she was very fond, and to restrain her from getting divorced from her unsatisfactory husband until she had established a relationship with a better man. (Freud, 1907b, p. 120)

Freud went on to diagnose his patient Ernst Lanzer's religious behaviour as symptomatic of conflict between repressed and unconscious hatred of his father and conscious love of him. This behaviour included Lanzer obsessively praying as a child. He also began obsessively praying again as an adult when it took longer and longer to complete because, said Freud,

> [S]omething always inserted itself into his pious phrases and turned them into their opposite. [...] [I]f he said, 'May God protect him', an evil spirit would hurriedly insinuate a 'not'. On one such occasion the idea occurred to him of cursing instead, for in that case, he thought, the contrary words would be sure to creep in. His original intention, which had been repressed by his praying, was forcing its way through in this last idea of his. In the end he found his way out of his embarrassment by giving up the prayers and replacing them by a short formula concocted out of the initial letters or syllables of various prayers. He then recited this formula so quickly that nothing could slip into it. (Freud, 1909b, p. 193)

To this Freud added evidence of similar conflict in Lanzer in a dream in which Freud's mother died and Lanzer could not decide whether or not to condole with him.

Unlike Lanzer, Freud was not conflicted about religion. He denounced 'religious inhibition of thought [...] brought into play by education' (Freud, 1910b, p. 79); described as delusional the religious preoccupations of Schreber (see pp. 78, 81 above); deplored an 'ascetic current in Christianity' whereby monks became 'entirely occupied with the struggle against libidinal temptation' (Freud, 1912a, p. 188); and diagnosed the religious rituals of his patient Sergei Pankejeff as symptoms of 'obsessional' neurosis (Freud, 1918b, p. 61).

'[W]hy was it that none of all the pious ever discovered psychoanalysis? Why did it have to wait for a completely godless Jew?' he asked his pastor friend, Oskar Pfister (Freud, 1918c, p. 63). In an address to a Jewish organization, the Society of B'nai B'rith, Freud acknowledged,

> What bound me to Jewry was [...] neither faith nor national pride, for I have always been an unbeliever and was brought up without religion though not without a respect for what are called the 'ethical' standards of human civilization. (Freud, 1926, p. 273)

Freud mused more about religion in his book *The Future of an Illusion*, which he seemingly addressed to Pfister. In it he argued that in ancient times people sought to humanize natural forces by thinking of them as gods. He likened this to children experiencing their parents, especially their fathers, as all-powerful protectors whom they also fear. This experience persists, he maintained, in the religious belief that

> Over each of us there watches a benevolent Providence which is only seemingly stern and which will not suffer us to become a plaything of the over-mighty and pitiless forces of nature. (Freud, 1927a, p. 19)

'[L]ike the obsessional neuroses of childhood', Freud speculated, perhaps thinking of Sergei Pankejeff's religious rituals (see p. 88 above), religion developed historically 'out of the Oedipus complex [...] relation to the father'. To this he added criticism of religious teaching for weakening the educational development of children. As remedy to religion causing inhibitions in children, as it had in Sergei's case, he urged its withdrawal from education.

Freud also countered religion with science. Through 'its numerous important successes', he concluded, science has proved itself, unlike religion, to be 'no illusion' (Freud, 1927a, pp. 43, 55).

Critics of Freud's resulting book included the celebrated French writer Romain Rolland. He regretted that Freud said nothing in this book about the source of religious feeling in the 'oceanic' experience of 'something limitless, unbounded'. Quoting this in his next book, Freud said he was not aware of any such oceanic feeling in himself. He redescribed it as involving 'being one with the external world as a whole', and psychoanalyzed this experience as rooted in the breast-feeding baby's feeling of oneness with its mother's body (Freud, 1930, p. 65).

He also described this feeling as recurring in the lover experiencing oneness with their beloved. This has inspired many subsequent psychoanalysts and psychoanalytically minded writers (see e.g. Milner, 1952; Stokes, 1955; Kristeva, 1982). Freud, however, dismissed the oceanic feeling of oneness as a source of religion.

Instead, on the basis of his clinically derived, father-centred psychoanalytic theory, he reported that, for him,

> The derivation of religious needs from the infant's helplessness and the longing for the father aroused by it seems to me incontrovertible, especially since the feeling is not simply prolonged from childhood days, but is permanently sustained by fear of the superior power of Fate. I cannot think of any need in childhood as strong as the need for a father's protection. Thus the part played by the oceanic feeling, which might seek something like the restoration of limitless narcissism, is ousted from a place in the foreground. (Freud, 1930, p. 72)

As for 'the oceanic feeling', he dismissed it as 'a first attempt at a religious consolation' and as a way of 'disclaiming the danger which the ego recognizes as threatening it from the external world' (Freud, 1930, p. 72). He nevertheless wrote more about religion, not least in his 1939 book, *Moses and Monotheism* (of which more on pp. 182, 187 below).

SUMMARY: Like his father, Freud was opposed to religious observances and rituals. He linked them psychoanalytically with obsessional symptoms, explained religious belief in terms of the child's experience of its father as all-powerful protector, and regarded religion as a consoling defence against danger.

SOCIOLOGY

In psychoanalytic sociology, Freud is perhaps best known for his book *Civilization and Its Discontents*, first published in 1930. But he also wrote about sociological issues, at least about issues of social class, long before that.

This included his explaining why, although child sexual abuse might be frequent in the working class, it more often causes psychological ills – at least hysteria – in the middle class. Freud (1896b) attributed this to hysteria only resulting from such abuse if, after being recognized as sexual after puberty, it is thereby rendered traumatic and repressed such that it is rendered unconscious and converted into the bodily symptoms of hysteria.

He also drew attention to ways in which middle class girls in his time were kept in ignorance of their sexual feelings. This and other factors contributed, he said, to their becoming sexually unhappy as adults and to their transferring the need for love from their husbands onto their infants, whose 'sexual precocity' they thereby awakened (Freud, 1908d, p. 202).

In lectures about psychoanalysis, Freud said more about the sexual repression of middle class girls. In doing so he contrasted two imagined girls, one working class, the other middle class. After their sexual games together as children – games which include watching each other urinate and defecate, and stimulating each other's genitals – the working class girl, free from repressing the memory of these games, grows up, he imagined, to be relatively free from neurosis. Not so the middle class girl of whom he said,

> At an early stage and while she is still a child she will get an idea that she has done something wrong; after a short time, but perhaps only after a severe struggle, she will give up her masturbatory satisfaction, but she will nevertheless still have some sense of oppression about her. When in her later girlhood she is in a position to learn something of human sexual intercourse, she will turn away from it with unexplained disgust and prefer to remain in ignorance. And now she will probably be subject to a fresh emergence of an irresistible pressure to masturbate of which she will not dare to complain. During the years in which she should exercise a feminine attraction upon some man, a neurosis breaks out in her which cheats her of marriage and her hopes in life. If after this an analysis succeeds in gaining an insight into her neurosis, it will turn out that the well-brought-up, intelligent and high-minded girl has completely repressed her sexual impulses, but that these, unconscious to her, are still attached to her petty experiences with her childhood friend. (Freud, 1915-1917, pp. 353–354)

In his later writings Freud said little about such social class issues. Instead, in an essay written during the 1914–1918 World War, he contrasted 'primitive' and 'civilized' societies. The latter involve, he said, 'high norms of moral conduct'. These entail, he maintained, 'much renunciation of instinctual satisfaction' and, he added, 'forbidden' use by the individual of 'the immense advantages to be gained by the practice of lying and deception in the competition with his fellow-men' (Freud, 1915e, p. 276).

Freud reiterated themes from this essay in launching psychoanalytic sociology with his 1930 book, *Civilization and Its Discontents*. In it he wrote about ways in which we are threatened by the forces of nature and by our relations with other people. These threats, he argued, are fended off by sublimation of the sexual drive in artistic creation, scientific investigation, and in enjoyment of works of art and beauty. They are also fended off, he added, by the delusions of madness and religion.

Yet, Freud pessimistically maintained, civilization also causes us 'misery'. True, he acknowledged, civilization has resulted in immense technological advance and control of nature. It has also encouraged intellectual, scientific, and artistic achievement and the development of moral ideals. Yet, in replacing 'the power of the individual' with '[t]he power of the community', he argued, civilization restricts individual 'satisfaction' and 'liberty' (Freud, 1930, pp. 86, 95).

Particularly significant for Freud was the extent to which civilization is constructed at the cost of repressing the sexual drive of its individual members. This repression is nevertheless necessary due to communal life being formed, he maintained, on the basis of the power of love and the need to work binding members of society together.

Yet society restricts the love life of its individual members. It does this with its taboo on incest; its refusal to acknowledge the sexuality of children; its taboo on sex outside marriage; and with its characterization of non-genital sexuality and homosexuality as perverse. It was precisely the psychological ills caused by such restrictions that largely contributed to Freud founding psychoanalysis. Nevertheless, he now insisted, these restrictions help bind individuals together in society.

He was also mindful, however, that we are not only driven by a life-enhancing, constructive, sexual drive or instinct. He called it Eros. We are also driven, he maintained, by a destructive death instinct, Thanatos, about which he had first written (see p. 135 above) in seeking to understand the repeated nightmares of victims of the 1914–1918 World War.

Now in *Civilization and Its Discontents* he called this instinct or drive, insofar as it is directed at the external world, an instinct of aggression. As a result of this instinct, he argued,

> [Our] neighbour is for [us] not only a potential helper or sexual object, but also someone who tempts [us] to satisfy [our] aggressiveness on him, to exploit his capacity for work without compensation, to use him sexually without his consent, to seize his possessions, to humiliate him, to cause him pain, to torture and to kill him. (Freud, 1930, p. 111)

Our instinct of aggression, together with our assumption that fellow citizens are driven by the same instinct, threatens civilization with disintegration. On this basis Freud was sceptical about communism with its belief that, as he put it,

> [M]an is wholly good and well-disposed to his neighbour; but the institution of private property has corrupted his nature. The ownership of private wealth gives the individual power, and with it the temptation to ill-treat his neighbour; while the man who is excluded from possession is bound to rebel in hostility against his oppressor. If private property were abolished, all wealth held in common, and everyone allowed to share in the enjoyment of it, ill-will and hostility would disappear among men. Since everyone's needs would be satisfied, no one would have any reason to regard another as his enemy; all would willingly undertake the work that was necessary. (Freud, 1930, p. 113)

Doubtless abolition of private property, as advocated by communism, would reduce one of the causes of human aggression, Freud acknowledged. But, he maintained, this would in no way alter the misuse of aggression for the purpose of power and influence.

While Eros is beneficial to civilization in binding people together, he went on in Hobbesian vein, Thanatos fuels 'hostility of each against all and of all against each' (Freud, 1930, p. 122). How, then, is this anti-social instinct of hostility and aggression managed? In answering this question, Freud drew on his previously developed theory of the superego as an agency in the ego resulting from identifying with one's parents, particularly the father and the social rules he represents.

Regarding the superego as an agent of conscience and the sense of guilt guarding and controlling aggression between individual members of society, Freud said of its determinants

> [T]he child's revengeful aggressiveness will be in part determined by the amount of punitive aggression which he expects from his father. Experience shows, however, that the severity of the super-ego which

> a child develops in no way corresponds to the severity of treatment which he has himself met with. The severity of the former seems to be independent of the latter. A child who has been very leniently brought up can acquire a very strict conscience. But it would also be wrong to exaggerate this independence; it is not difficult to convince oneself that severity of upbringing does also exert a strong influence on the formation of the child's super-ego. (Freud, 1930, p. 130)

It is through reinforcing a more or less unconscious sense of guilt, bred by the father-based superego that, said Freud, civilization counters the disruption of its erotically based close-knit character caused by the instinct of aggression. It is this sense of guilt, he maintained, that is the price we pay for civilization in the loss of happiness. The work of psychoanalytic treatment accordingly included for him, at this stage in its development, enabling patients to become conscious of their otherwise unconscious sense of guilt and reduce the harshness of its superego agent's 'demands' on the ego (Freud, 1930, p. 143).

Not long after this was published, and the same year as Adolf Hitler was appointed chancellor of Germany, the psychoanalyst Wilhelm Reich (1933) attributed the rise of fascism at that time to the sexual repression exercised by Germany's working class families on their children. Also in the 1930s, sociologists in the Institute of Social Research in Frankfurt attributed the rise of fascism in Germany to families imbuing their offspring with superego identification with the authority of the father, thereby predisposing them to submit to fascist authoritarianism.

This was followed, after the end of the 1939–1945 World War, by sociologist émigrés from Hitler's fascist Germany using Freud's theory of the superego as a means of understanding persisting fascist, authoritarian, and anti-Semitic traits in those they studied. Particularly notable and influential in this respect was the 1950 book *The Authoritarian Personality*, by Theodor Adorno and his colleagues.

In subsequent years, some social commentators – notably Christopher Lasch (1979) – expressed regret about declining interest in the superego and in the inner world more generally. Sociological interest in psychoanalysis, however, has not entirely declined. Certainly Freud's psychoanalytic work informs ongoing sociological discussion of gender and race issues (as explained in Chapters 29 and 30 below).

Thanks to the work of Joanna Ryan (2017), there has also been a revival of psychoanalytic interest in the issue of social class to which, as I indicated at the start of this chapter, Freud related the psychodynamic defence of repression. Psychoanalytic ideas also inform psychosocial studies departments at various colleges and universities in the UK including Birkbeck and the University of Essex. Recent publications combining psychoanalysis with sociology include David Morgan's 2019 edited collection, *The Unconscious in Social and Political Life*, and Bernard Lahire's 2020 book, *The Sociological Interpretation of Dreams*.

> SUMMARY: In his early work Freud emphasized differences between the working and the middle class regarding the repression of sexuality. However, he arguably launched psychoanalytic sociology with his later account in his 1930 book, *Civilization and Its Discontents*, of the patriarchal superego as source of the control of the otherwise disintegrating social effect of aggression, this being followed by further works combining psychoanalysis with sociology not least today.

29

GENDER POLITICS

Other areas beyond the clinical practice of psychoanalysis influenced by Freud's work include what is now called gender politics. They comprise both feminist issues and issues currently described as lesbian, gay, bisexual, and trans (LGBT).

FEMINIST ISSUES

Freud himself was no feminist. He was conservative in his attitude to women's proper social role. During his courtship of his fiancée, Martha Bernays, in November 1883 he told her,

> Law and custom have much to give women that has been withheld from them, but the[ir] position [...] will surely be what it is: in youth an adored darling and in mature years a loved wife. (In Jones, 1953, p. 193)

Freud was nevertheless sympathetic to the plight of young middle class women.

Together with his colleague Josef Breuer, he argued that these women's 'needlework and similar occupations' made them prone to the day-dreaming 'hypnoid' states of mind causing hysteria (Breuer & Freud, 1893, p. 13). He deplored the sexual repression of middle class women contributing to their becoming neurotic (see pp. 174–175 above). He described as 'bondage' the rights exercised by men over their wives. And he drew attention to what he described as 'narcissism of minor differences' contributing to men 'despising' women (Freud, 1918a, pp. 193,199).

Yet he also reduced feminist struggle against what we now might describe as sexism to an aspect of penis envy. Examples include his saying of his eighteen-year-old patient Marguerite Csonka,

> A spirited girl, always ready for romping and fighting, she was not at all prepared to be second to her slightly older brother; after inspecting his genital organs she had developed a pronounced envy for the penis, and the thoughts derived from this envy still continued to fill her mind. She was in fact a feminist; she felt it to be unjust that girls should not enjoy the same freedom as boys, and rebelled against the lot of woman in general. (Freud, 1920b, p. 169)

The psychoanalyst and feminist Karen Horney was appalled by Freud's penis envy account of the psychological development of the girl in becoming a woman. It was no different, she said, from the attitude of the little boy who regards the girl as 'castrated'; believes that she 'has suffered punishment that also threatens him'; and is 'unable to imagine how the girl can ever get over [her penis] envy'. If the girl envies the boy his penis, Horney maintained, this is only because she wants to defend with masculinity against her guilt-making feminine Oedipal desire for her father. Furthermore this defence is, she added, 'reinforced and supported by the actual disadvantages under which women labor in social life' and by 'the greater importance attaching to the male sociologically' (Horney, 1926, pp. 57–58, 69).

Melanie Klein (1928) also took issue with Freud's Oedipus complex theory, but not on feminist grounds. Her child patients' transference experience of her, arguably on account of her sex, as a maternal figure convinced her that the superego begins pre-Oedipally with the infant identifying with the mother as a hostile figure retaliating against its attack on her sexuality.

Freud (1931) in turn applauded the women psychoanalysts Helene Deutsch and Jeanne Lampl-de Groot who, through attending to their patients' transference experience of them as mother figures, discovered more than he had about the pre-Oedipal determinants of our psychology. Why, though, had Freud overlooked these determinants? In answering this question he replied,

> Everything in the sphere of this first attachment to the mother seemed to me so difficult to grasp in analysis – so grey with age and shadowy and almost impossible to revivify – that it was as if it had succumbed to an especially inexorable repression. But perhaps I gained this impression because the women who were in analysis with me were able to cling to the very attachment to the father in which they had taken refuge from the early phase that was in question. (Freud, 1931, p. 226)

'I do *not* like to be the mother in the transference', Freud admitted to his patient Hilda Doolittle, '– it always surprises and shocks me a little. I feel so very masculine' (Doolittle, 1933, pp. 146–147).

He also persisted in his patriarchalism and celebration of men in contrast to women. Examples include his saying in almost his last book, *Moses and Monotheism*,

> An advance in intellectuality consists in deciding against direct sense-perception in favour of what are known as the higher intellectual processes – that is, memories, reflections and inferences. It consists, for instance, in deciding that paternity is more important than maternity, although it cannot, like the latter, be established by the evidence of the senses, and that for that reason the child should bear his father's name and be his heir. (Freud, 1939, pp. 117–118)

It was in terms of this advance in intellectuality that he celebrated what he described as 'the victory of patriarchy' (Freud, 1939, p. 118).

In subsequent years, feminists and many others have criticized Freud for his patriarchalism and penis envy account of women's psychology. Some have nevertheless defended this account. Particularly influential in this respect has been Juliet Mitchell's insistence that, as she puts it,

> However it may have been used, psychoanalysis is not a recommendation *for* a patriarchal society, but an analysis *of* one. If we are interested in understanding and challenging the oppression of women, we cannot afford to neglect it. (Mitchell, 1974, p. xv, italics in original)

This, however, does not excuse the fact that, despite the contribution to psychoanalysis of women psychoanalysts, Juliet Mitchell included, no woman was made president of the International Psychoanalytic Association for over a century after its foundation in 1910. It was only in 2019 that for the first time a woman, Virginia Ungar, was appointed to this position. This is a feminist issue. So too are LGBT issues, to which I turn next.

LGBT ISSUES

Although Freud argued that the infant is initially bisexual – in that it has both active and passive, masculine and feminine aims – this did not stop him regarding bisexuality as a sexual perversion. He also depicted Schreber's homosexual desire as the pathological effect of regression to narcissism, and as resulting from the defences of repression, reversal, and projection (see p. 80 above).

Furthermore, Freud described the homosexual or lesbian form of the Oedipus complex as 'negative' in contrast to what he described as its 'positive' heterosexual form (Freud, 1923a, p. 33). With this heterosexist attitude, as the psychoanalytic psychotherapists Noreen O'Connor and Joanna Ryan (1993) point out, Freud equated sexual desire for someone the same sex as themselves as entailing that their gender – masculine or feminine – is the negative or opposite of their biological sex – male or female.

Despite his heterosexist attitude in this respect, Freud did not regard gay or lesbian sexuality – homosexuality, he called it – as in itself requiring psychoanalytic treatment. Anyway, he pointed out,

> [T]o undertake to convert a fully developed homosexual into a heterosexual does not offer much more prospect of success than the reverse, except that for good practical reasons the latter is never attempted. (Freud, 1920b, p. 151)

Freud also famously told a mother worried about her son being homosexual,

> Homosexuality is assuredly no advantage, but it is nothing to be ashamed of, no vice, no degradation, it cannot be classified as an illness; we consider it to be a variation of the sexual function produced by a certain arrest of sexual development. Many highly respectable individuals of ancient and modern times have been homosexuals, several of the greatest men among them (Plato, Michelangelo, Leonardo da Vinci, etc.). It is a great injustice to persecute homosexuality as a crime and cruelty too. (Freud, 1935, n.p.)

Nevertheless, during my psychoanalytic training in the 1990s, homosexuality and lesbianism were regarded as conditions needing psychoanalytic treatment. Furthermore homosexual and lesbian patients were described as not really homosexual or lesbian, whereas I never heard a heterosexual patient described as not really heterosexual.

At that time the British Psychoanalytic Society and other psychoanalytic training organizations discriminated against taking on homosexuals and lesbians as trainees. This only ended in 2012 when the British Psychoanalytic Council (BPC) agreed to overturn this discrimination. In doing so, reports Juliet Newbigin (2015), the BPC insisted that homosexuality and lesbianism are not evidence of psychological disturbance or problematic, arrested, or fixated psychosexual development.

As well as being less sexist and heterosexist than in the past, psychoanalysts today are also more liberal about trans issues. This is evident, for example, in accounts by the psychoanalyst Alessandra Lemma (2013, 2018) of her work with patients with varying trans identities.

SUMMARY: Freud's account of feminism and women's psychology in terms of penis envy has been variously criticized and defended. His sympathetic approach to homosexuality has also been noted. So too have varying discriminatory and non-discriminatory attitudes, past and present, of psychoanalysts to what are described as lesbian, gay, bisexual, and trans issues today.

30

RACISM

[Handwritten annotations: "Of the time" with arrow; "Sexist / Racist / Reflected appropriate cultural values?"]

In keeping with the colonialist attitudes of his class and time, Freud was racist. He described colonized people as savage and primitive, and he likened them to infants and young children. He also went along with colonialism and racial prejudice in writing about 'wars between […] primitive and […] civilized peoples' and between 'races […] divided by the colour of their skin' (Freud, 1915e, p. 276).

He was, however, appalled by anti-Semitic racism and by his father's subservience to it (see p. 4 above). He also treated racism, like neurotic symptoms, as something that needed psychoanalytic understanding. Having psychoanalysed men despising women as the effect of 'narcissism of minor differences' (see p. 181 above), he went on to argue that narcissism likewise contributes to the fact that, as he put it,

> Closely related races keep one another at arm's length; the South German cannot endure the North German, the Englishman casts every kind of aspersion upon the Scot, the Spaniard despises the Portuguese. […] [G]reater differences […] lead to an almost insuperable repugnance, such as the Gallic people feel for the German, the Aryan for the Semite, and the white races for the coloured. (Freud, 1921, p. 101)

He nevertheless objected, not surprisingly, to anti-Semitic racism resulting in his being expected, as a university student, 'to feel himself to be "inferior and an alien" because he was a Jew'. He also suspected that opposition to psychoanalysis, framed in terms of his being 'a citizen of Vienna', was due to his being 'Jewish' (Freud, 1925c, pp. 9, 39–40). To this he added speculation about increasing anti-Semitism at the time of the Nazi party's rise to power in Germany as a corollary of its dream of 'world-domination' (Freud, 1930, p. 115).

After the annexation by Hitler's Germany of Austria in March 1938, Freud – together with his wife, Martha, their daughter, Anna, their maid, his dog, and his doctor – were helped by one of his former psychoanalytic patients, Princess Marie Bonaparte, to leave Vienna early that June for Paris. From there they went to London where he addressed the issue of anti-Semitism in completing his book *Moses and Monotheism*.

Anti-Semitism was an issue in Britain. Examples included the October 1936 Cable Street riots in London. Two years later, in reply to the editor of the magazine *Time and Tide*, inviting him to contribute to a discussion of anti-Semitism, Freud said of the problem it had posed him and psychoanalysis,

> I came to Vienna as a child of 4 from a small town in Moravia. After 78 years of assiduous work I had to leave my home, saw the Scientific Society I had founded, dissolved, our institutions destroyed, our Printing Press ('Verlag') taken over by the invaders, the books I had published confiscated or reduced to pulp, my children expelled from their professions. (Freud, 1938, p. 301)

He was also struck by the editor's account of the growth at that time of anti-Semitism in Britain.

Anti-Semitism persisted following Freud's death in Hampstead on 23 September 1939. It also persisted following the end of the 1939–1945 World War. Post-war studies of anti-Semitism drew on Freud's theories. They included a report by Nathan Ackerman and Marie Jahoda (1950) of psychoanalytic observations regarding anti-Semitism as a defence against anxiety.

Much better known are the findings about anti-Semitism reported by Theodor Adorno and his colleagues in the United States. In their book *The Authoritarian Personality*, they forged – on the basis of interview data, responses to an anti-Semitism questionnaire, and other findings – a psychoanalytic account of the developmental psychology precursors of anti-Semitism. In particular they argued that those who had had an excessively harsh and punitive upbringing were likely defensively to displace anger against their parents onto anger with Jews.

The psychologist Stephen Frosh (2016) adds to these and other findings regarding anti-Semitism. He argues that it involves the psychodynamic defence of projection whereby, in his view, anti-Semites project unconscious disturbance in themselves onto Jews as hate objects or figures.

Long before that, the black psychiatrist Frantz Fanon (1952) used Freud's account of the related psychodynamic defences of introjection and identification (see e.g. p. 130 above) in arguing that black people often find themselves identifying with, and introjecting the projections into them of what white people dislike in themselves. As a result, argued Fanon, many black people, consciously or unconsciously, wish they were white.

Some are critical of those who reduce racism to psychology, specifically to a binary process of projection and introjection, thereby neglecting historical, social, and other factors causing racism (see e.g. Ward, 1997). Others are impressed by Fanon's use of the defence of introjection as means of explaining some of the psychological effects of racism on its target people.

A related approach is adopted by the Asian psychoanalyst Fakhry Davids, from South Africa and living in London. Whereas Fanon highlighted ways in which the targets of racism identify with, and defend against the racist's projections onto them. Davids also writes about ways in which white people introject and use racism as a psychological retreat from, and defence against anxiety.

He illustrates this with an occurrence in his psychoanalytic treatment of a white psychoanalytic patient, Mr A. Of this occurrence Davids says,

> During his third psychoanalytic appointment Mr A described an incident in which, enraged with his mother communicating his father's fury with him for failing to renew their car insurance, Mr A became convinced when he heard an unfamiliar sound coming from his own new and unfamiliar car that it was about to explode. He also became convinced that his mother was dead. Davids interpreted this to Mr A as indicating that he wanted to warn Davids about his 'enormous rage' and fear that, 'were this touched in his therapy', Davids would not be able to cope with it. This interpretation infuriated Mr A. Responding angrily to it, he complained that 'no one ever wanted to know about [his] enormous, ugly, horrible rage'. All they wanted, he furiously said, was for him to be reasonable and 'settle down nicely'. (Adapted from Davids, 2011, pp. 22–23)

Why this rage? Because, says Davids, Mr A had projected his problem with rage and other rejected aspects of himself onto Davids as a brown-skinned foreigner struggling to find acceptance in hostile and racist Britain. As such, argues Davids, Mr A retreated in his fury into an introjected and defensive racist organization constructed to protect himself against terrifying anxiety and against fear of being dependent on other people by projecting this anxiety onto Davids.

SUMMARY: Although Freud was racist, he also psychoanalysed anti-Semitic and anti-black racism as the effect of what he described as narcissism of minor differences. More recently racism has been understood psychoanalytically in terms of Freud's account of the defences of projection, identification, and introjection.

CONCLUSIONS TO PART VI

In an interview for BBC radio in December 1938, some months before his death far from Vienna, where he had lived almost all his life, Freud recalled,

> I started my professional activity as a neurologist trying to bring relief to my neurotic patients. Under the influence of an older friend [Josef Breuer] and by my own efforts, I discovered some important new facts about the unconscious in psychic life, the role of instinctual urges, and so on. Out of these findings grew a new science, psychoanalysis, a part of psychology, and a new method of treatment of the neuroses. I had to pay heavily for this bit of good luck. People did not believe in my facts and thought my theories unsavoury. Resistance was strong and unrelenting. In the end I succeeded in acquiring pupils and building up an International Psychoanalytic Association. But the struggle is not yet over. (Anon, 2012, n.p.)

The struggle to secure and develop Freud's psychoanalytic insights did not end with his death. It continues largely because of their importance as means of understanding unconscious–conscious dynamics in everyday life, of understanding psychosexual development, and as a basis for treating psychological ills. More than this, through extending psychoanalysis beyond its clinical practice, Freud remains today a continuing influence on art, literature, and film, and on anthropology, religion, sociology, and on gender and anti-racist politics too.

GLOSSARY

Further details of the meaning of Freudian, post-Freudian, and other terms relevant to this book can be found in *A Critical Dictionary of Psychoanalysis* by Charles Rycroft; *The Language of Psycho-Analysis* by Jean Laplanche and Jean-Bertram Pontalis; and in *A-Z of Psychodynamic Practice* by Jeffrey Longhofer.

Abreaction Discharge of emotion evoked by a trauma which is otherwise unconscious because, according to Breuer (1895b), it first occurred when the patient was in a hypnoid or day-dreaming state of mind, or, according to Freud (1895c), because it has been repressed.

Aggression An externally directed derivative, according to Freud (1930), of the death instinct.

Ambivalence Simultaneous experience of contradictory feelings – specifically love and hate – for one and the same person or object.

Anal character Freud (1908c) described this character type – involving obstinacy, orderliness, and parsimony (meanness) – as rooted in the anal stage of infant or early child development.

Anal-sadism Illustrative of this state of mind for Freud (1918b) was his patient Sergei Pankejeff, when he was a three-year-old, being cruel to small animals, catching flies and pulling off their wings, crushing beetles underfoot, imagining beating large animals such as horses, and tormenting his nursemaid – sadistic behaviour which Freud connected with Sergei's later predilection for anal intercourse.

Anal stage Period of early childhood psychosexual development in which, according to Freud (e.g. 1905b, 1915–1917), the sexual drive centres on pleasurable anal sensations.

Anxiety An experience resulting, according to Freud (1926), from consciously perceived danger or from something repressed and unconscious.

Attachment A term introduced into post-Freudian psychoanalysis to highlight the importance for 'mental health' of the infant's and young child's 'experience of a warm, intimate, and continuous relationship' with the person by whom they are first mothered 'in which both find satisfaction and enjoyment' (Bowlby, 1953, p.13).

Autoerotism Freud used this term to refer to pleasure derived from one's own body as in thumbsucking or masturbation.

Bipolar Disorder 1 The *DSM-5* defines this disorder as a severe form of Bipolar Disorder 2. Bipolar Disorder 1 involves a manic episode as well as at least three of the following symptoms: increased talkativeness, self-esteem or grandiosity; decreased need for sleep; increased goal-directed activity, energy level, or irritability; racing thoughts; poor attention; increased risk-taking (spending money, risky sexual behaviour, etc.).

Bisexuality Freud (e.g. 1931) equated this with what he described as the masculine and feminine, active and passive sexual desire of very young children, both male and female.

Castration complex This is exacerbated in boys, according to Freud, by their attributing lack of a penis in girls to it having been cut off, this resulting in the boy's fear that he might likewise lose his penis. Freud also sometimes described penis envy in girls as the female version of the boy's castration complex.

Cathartic treatment Means by which, said Breuer and Freud (1893), patients are enabled under hypnosis to re-experience and thereby purge or abreact the traumatically caused emotions producing their symptoms of hysteria.

Cathexes A term used by Freud (e.g. 1914c) to refer to investments of libido in other people or objects as he also called them.

Condensation Freud (e.g. 1900, 1901a) described condensation as an aspect of the dream-work whereby several elements of the latent or unconscious dream are combined together to form a single element in the consciously remembered manifest dream.

Consciousness Aspect of the mind contrasted by Freud (e.g. 1915b) with what is repressed and unconscious.

Conversion Term used by Freud (1895c) to describe the process whereby a repressed idea is transformed into a bodily symptom of hysteria.

Countertransference An experience described by Freud (1912b) as evoked in psychoanalysts by their patients.

Day's residues Elements from the previous day which, according to Freud (1900), connected with a more or less unconscious wish, evoke a dream.

Death instinct A drive which Freud (1920) postulated as seeking to reduce stimulation to zero through, for instance, repeating traumatic experiences until they no longer have any stimulating effect.

Defence mechanisms For Freud these included the psychological defences of repression, projection, introjection, or identification as means of keeping unwanted experience out of conscious awareness.

Deferred action Freud (1895a) described this as a process whereby a memory trace of an earlier event is reactivated and given new meaning by a later event.

Delusion Term used to refer to a belief which is both untrue and a fixed idea which cannot be influenced by logic or evidence. Freud (1911b) includes examples in his account of Schreber's schizophrenia.

Denial In psychoanalysis this includes a defence mechanism whereby painful experience or an impulse or aspect of the self is negated.

Depression A gloomy state of mind, a severe form of which was referred to by Freud (1917) as melancholia. It can alternate with mania in the condition once diagnosed as manic-depressive psychosis and now diagnosed by the *DSM-5* as Bipolar Disorder 1.

DSM-5 *Diagnostic and Statistical Manual of Mental Disorders, Fifth Edition* of the American Psychiatric Association.

Disavowal Term used by Freud (1927b) to refer to a defence involving refusal to recognize the reality of a traumatic perception, in particular the perception that women do not have a penis.

Displacement Term used by Freud (e.g. 1900) whereby emphasis is defensively shifted from a significant to a relatively insignificant item in, for instance, a remembered dream.

Dissociative Identity Disorder (DID) The *DSM-5* defines this disorder in terms of the presence of two or more distinct identities or personality states in the patient, each state having its own relatively enduring pattern of perceiving, relating to, and thinking about the environment and themselves.

Dream-work Process whereby, according to Freud (e.g. 1900), latent and unconscious wishes fuelling dreams are transformed into their manifest and consciously recalled form through condensation, displacement, representation, and secondary revision.

Economic model In psychoanalysis this refers to Freud's focus on the libido's 'economic' investments or cathexes of others as its objects (Freud, 1915c, p.181).

Ego Freud initially equated the ego with the conscious mind. He later regarded it as partially unconscious. Later still he described it as 'part of the id which has been modified by the direct influence of the external world' (Freud, 1923a, p.25).

Ego psychology A version of psychoanalysis which developed following publication of Freud's (1923) id-ego-superego model of the mind.

Ego ideal A term used by Freud (1914c, 1917, 1921) in writing about narcissism, melancholia, and about group psychology. It refers to an aspect of the ego to which the individual tries to aspire or conform. It is a precursor of the superego terminology introduced by Freud in 1923.

Electra complex Freud explicitly rejected this term used by Jung (e.g. 1913a) and by others to refer to the female form of the Oedipus complex.

Eros Name of the Greek god of sexual love used by Freud (e.g. 1920a, 1930) to characterize the constructive life instinct in contrast to the destructive death instinct to which he gave the name Thanatos.

Erotogenic zone A term used by Freud (e.g. 1905b) to refer to areas of the body – specifically oral, anal, or genital areas – from which sexual pleasure is derived.

Exhibitionism Passive sexual pleasure in being watched by others. Freud (e.g. 1905b) contrasted it with the active sexual pleasure of voyeurism.

Fantasy A term, sometimes spelt 'phantasy', referring in Freud's work to the product of conscious or unconscious imagination.

Fetishism A perversion which, according to Freud (1905b, 1915–1917), requires the presence of a particular thing or object as precondition for the arousal of sexual desire.

Fixation Freud (1905b) used this term to refer to the sexual drive or libido becoming stuck at a particular stage of its development in infancy or early childhood.

Free association Describing this as the 'fundamental rule of psycho-analysis', Freud insisted that patients in psychoanalytic treatment say whatever occurs to them however irrelevant or unpleasant it may seem (Freud, 1914a, p.147).

Gain, primary and secondary Distinction made by Freud (e.g. 1905a) between the unconscious wish-fulfilling primary process hallucinatory gain accruing from neurotic symptoms and the conscious secondary process actual gain accruing from these symptoms in so far as they result, for instance, in the patient being looked after by others.

Genital stage A stage in psychosexual development in which, according to Freud (e.g. 1905b, 1915–1917), infants derive pleasure from genital stimulation. Since, according to Freud (1923b), only one genital, namely the penis, features in the infant's psychology at this stage of their psychosexual development, he renamed it the phallic stage.

Guilt According to Freud (1923a), the sense of guilt arises from tension between the ego and the superego which, through its self-punishing form can cause the psychoanalytic patient's negative therapeutic reaction against recovering from the psychological ills for which they are being psychoanalytically treated.

Hypnoid state A term used by Breuer (1895b) to refer to a more or less unconscious day-dreaming state of mind akin to that produced by hypnosis resulting in its contents remaining unconscious.

Hysteria A condition now rarely if ever diagnosed. It was initially regarded as a condition only affecting women. It was later diagnosed by the neurologist and anatomical pathologist Martin Charcot as caused by psychological trauma and as occurring in both sexes. To his account of hysteria Freud (1895c) added that it involves the conversion of repressed and unconscious sexual feeling into bodily symptoms.

Id An aspect of the mind derived by Freud (1923a) from Groddeck's account of the It. Freud used the term 'id' to designate the unconscious reservoir of the drives or instincts fuelling the ego and superego and subject to their control.

Identification Examples for Freud (1917) included melancholic or severely depressed patients defensively identifying in their ego with those whom they have loved, hated, and lost. Freud (1923a) argued that identification with parents and others in our lives is the source of the ego and superego.

Infantile amnesia The term used by Freud (e.g. 1905b) to refer to the process whereby we repress and forget the sexual wishes of our earliest months and years.

Instinct A biologically determined drive which Freud (e.g. 1915a) emphasized can vary in its biological source (e.g. oral, anal, genital), aim (e.g. passive or active), and object (e.g. part or whole, human or animal).

Interpretation The process in psychoanalysis whereby the latent or unconscious meaning of dreams, symptoms, and other psychological phenomena is translated into conscious, verbally expressed meaning.

Introjection Akin to identification, introjection refers to the process whereby experience of relations with others is internalized such that they become what have been described as object relations figures within the mind or inner world.

Latency The developmental period which, according to Freud (e.g. 1905b), is initiated by the five- or six-year-old repressing their previous sexual experience and desire prior to it being reawakened by puberty.

Latent content Freud (e.g. 1900) used this term to refer to the unconscious, wish-fulfilling thoughts fuelling dreams.

Libido A term used by Freud (e.g. 1915–1917) to refer to sexual energy which, he said, can vary in its object (e.g. male or female), aim (e.g. active or passive), and source (e.g. oral, anal, or genital).

Mania Symptoms of mania, alternating with depression, have been described by the *DSM-5* as including inflated self-esteem, decreased need for sleep, increased talkativeness, racing thoughts, and being easily distracted. Freud (1917) attributed these symptoms to the narcissism involved in melancholia with which mania sometimes alternates.

Manifest content Freud (e.g. 1900) used this term to refer to the content of the consciously recalled dream in contrast to its unconscious, wish-fulfilling, latent content.

Masochism Sexual pleasure in being subjected to cruelty. Freud (1905b) described masochism as the passive form of sadism.

Material reality Freud (e.g. 1915–1917) used this term to refer to external reality as opposed to internal, psychological reality.

Melancholia Severe depression involving, according to Freud (1917), defensive identification in the ego with someone who has been loved, hated, and lost.

Metapsychology A term used to refer to Freud's essays, published in 1915 and 1917, in which he consolidated and developed the theoretical underpinning of psychoanalysis.

Mourning Process following bereavement involving grief work during which, according to Freud (1917), the bereaved detach their libido bit by bit from the person who has died.

Narcissism Freud (1910b, 1911b, 1914c) described narcissism as a stage in psychosexual development in which the part-object, auto-erotic drives (oral, anal, genital) combine in the infant when it adopts itself as whole-object of its desire. This is succeeded developmentally, he said, by love and desire for others. He called this object-love.

Narcissus Freud (e.g. 1910b) derived the term 'narcissism' from the Greek myth about Narcissus falling in love with his reflection in a pool of water.

Negation Freud likened judgement about whether or not to negate and repress a thought to the infant judging whether something is good or bad by as it were saying to itself, 'I should like to eat this' or 'I should like to spit it out' (Freud, 1925a, p.237).

Negative therapeutic reaction Freud (1923a) used this term to describe patients who, due to the self-punishment resulting from their superego-caused unconscious sense of guilt, resist recovery from the psychological ills for which they seek psychoanalytic treatment.

Neurosis A condition which Freud (1915–1917) theorized as resulting from ego-libido conflict, and which Freud (1924) later theorized as resulting from conflict between the ego and the id.

Object-love Freud's (e.g. 1911b) term for love of others as opposed to narcissistic self-love.

Obsessional neurosis Freud developed at least three different accounts of obsessional neurosis. They include his attribution of obsessional rituals to sexual guilt (Freud, 1907b); his argument that the rat punishment obsession of his patient, Ernst Lanzer, was due to conflict between repressed and unconscious hatred of his father and conscious love of him (Freud, 1909b); and his account of the obsessional symptoms in childhood of his Wolf Man patient, Sergei Pankejeff, as defence against castration complex anxiety (Freud, 1918b).

Obsessive Compulsive Disorder (OCD) This is defined by the *DSM-5* in terms of the patient experiencing recurrent and persistent thoughts, urges, or impulses as intrusive and unwanted; which in most patients cause them marked anxiety or distress; and which they seek to counter with more or less repetitive compulsive thoughts or actions.

Oceanic feeling A sense of limitless oneness with the universe which Freud (1930) argued originates psychologically in the breast-feeding infant experiencing itself as one with its mother's body.

Oedipus complex A term introduced by Freud (1910) and used by him to refer to early childhood rivalry with one parent for sexual possession of the other parent.

Oral stage Freud (e.g. 1905b, 1915–1917) argued that this stage of psychosexual development is initiated in earliest infancy by the hungry baby sucking at the breast (or bottle) for milk, this leading to its autoerotic pleasure in sucking its lips, fingers, or thumb.

Paranoia Fear of others theorized by Freud (e.g. 1911b) as resulting from defensive repression and projection of hatred onto others with the result that they are experienced as persecuting and hating oneself.

Parapraxes Term used to refer to slips and errors many examples of which are described by Freud (1901b) in his book *The Psychopathology of Everyday Life*.

Penis envy An attitude Freud (e.g. 1905a, 1915–1917, 1925b) used to characterize the response of girls on first seeing the boy's penis. He sometimes referred to the girl's penis envy as her castration complex.

Perversion Term which Freud (1905b) argued is generally used to refer to any sexual activity not geared to result in heterosexual genital union.

Phallic stage Stage in psychosexual development which Freud (1923b) used in redescribing the genital stage because, he argued, this stage of psychosexual development involves only one genital, the penis.

Phantasy A term referring in Freud's work to the product of conscious or unconscious imagination or fantasy; and used by the psychoanalyst Melanie Klein and her followers, Susan Isaacs (1948) and Elizabeth Bott Spillius (2001), for example, to refer to fantasy which is unconscious.

Phobia Fear of a particular situation or object. Examples include Freud's (1909a) patient, four-year-old Hans, whose phobia of horses Freud psychoanalyzed as the effect of Hans displacing onto horses fear of his father and the anxiety-provoking wish that he would die.

Projection Freud (1911b) described this as a defence involving repressing and getting rid of the resulting unconscious feeling onto someone else. Examples for Freud (1913a) included Schreber projecting, or getting rid of, his hateful feelings onto his doctor, Flechsig, with the result that he experienced Flechsig as hatefully persecuting him.

Psychical reality Freud (e.g. 1915–1917) used this term to distinguish psychical or psychological from material reality. It corresponds to the distinction, now often made in psychoanalysis, between the inner and outer world.

Pleasure principle A wish-fulfilling primary mental process characterizing, according to Freud (1911a), the repressed unconscious mind in contrast to the reality-oriented secondary mental process of the conscious mind.

Polymorphous perverse disposition A trait attributed by Freud (1905b) to infants insofar as their oral, anal, and genital sexuality has a multiplicity of sources, aims, and objects.

Post-traumatic stress disorder (PTSD) The *DSM-5* defines this condition as resulting from direct exposure to, witnessing, or indirect exposure to trauma resulting in it being re-experienced in the form of unwanted upsetting memories, nightmares, flashbacks, or emotional distress or physical reaction after being exposed to reminders of the trauma involved.

Preconscious An aspect of mind described by Freud (1915–1917) as not repressed and unconscious but as registering inwardly and outwardly given experience in a form that is available to, but not presently in the conscious mind.

Pressure technique Freud (1895) described this technique whereby he pressurized patients to say whatever occurred to them when he pressed his hand on their head. It was a precursor of his later free association method of psychoanalysis.

Primal scene Freud (e.g. 1918b) used this term to refer to actual or imagined observation of parental sexual intercourse.

Primary gain Term used by Freud to refer to one of the 'motives of illness', namely the one which secures primary process, hallucinatory, wish fulfilment in contrast to the actual, secondary gain resulting, for instance, from people doing the patient's bidding on account of their illness (Freud, 1905a, p.42).

Primary process Freud (e.g. 1911a) contrasted primary process, wish-fulfilling, unconscious thinking with secondary process, reality-based, conscious thinking.

Projection Defensive process whereby rejected and repressed experience is expelled and located as coming from someone other than oneself. Examples for Freud (1911b) included Schreber projecting hatred onto his doctor, Flechsig, thus causing him to fear Flechsig as a hateful persecutor.

Psychical reality Freud (e.g. 1915–1917) used this term to distinguish psychological from physical reality. It corresponds to the distinction, now often made in psychoanalysis, between the inner and outer world.

Psychoanalysis A form of psychological treatment founded by Freud involving concepts of the repressed unconscious and psychosexual development which he and his followers extended in seeking to understand many other areas of human activity including art, literature, and film as well as anthropology, religion, sociology, gender politics, and racism.

Psychoanalyst A term now restricted in Britain to apply to anyone who has completed a recognized psychoanalytic training such as that provided by the Institute of Psychoanalysis in London.

Psychodynamics This word initially referred to Freud's (e.g. 1900) account of unconscious-conscious dynamics. It is now often used interchangeably with the term 'psychoanalysis'.

Psychosexual stages For Freud (1915–1917), these stages comprised oral, anal, genital, Oedipal, latency, and pubertal developments of the sexual drive or libido. Freud (1923b) renamed the genital stage the phallic stage.

Psychosis Freud (1924) characterized this psychological condition, on account of the delusions involved, as involving conflict between the ego and external reality.

Reaction-formation A defence, according to Freud, against an unacceptable impulse. Examples for Freud (e.g. 1908c) include defence against anal mess with exaggerated orderliness.

Reality principle Freud (1911a) contrasted this reality-based, secondary process principle with wish-fulfilling, pleasure principle governed, primary process thinking.

Regression Freud (e.g. 1915–1917) used this term to describe a defensive process whereby ego-libido conflict results in return of the libido to an earlier fixated stage in its development.

Repetition compulsion Concept used by Freud (1920a) to describe the repetition of trauma – the nightmares, for instance, repeating trauma suffered by victims of the 1914–1918 World War – a phenomenon which he attributed to the work of the death instinct.

Repression A defence which, according to Freud (e.g. 1915b), keeps or suppresses psychological phenomena with the result that they remain or become unconscious and may 'return' in the form of dreams, slips, jokes, neurotic symptoms, free associations, or, for instance, in the psychoanalytic patient's transference experience of their psychoanalyst.

Resistance Freud (e.g.1895c) used this term in seeking to understand why his patients failed to tell him whatever occurred in association to their psychological ills.

Reversal Freud (1911b) used this term to describe love turning into hate in, for instance, the case of Schreber's paranoia. Freud (1915a) also used this term to highlight the reversal of sadism into masochism, and of voyeurism into exhibitionism.

Sadism Sexual pleasure derived from being cruel to others. Freud (1905b) described it as the active form of the passive sexual pleasure derived from masochism.

Schizophrenia The *DSM-5* defines this condition as diagnosable provided the patient has experienced at least two of the following symptoms – delusions, hallucinations, or disorganized speech – for at least a month.

Screen memory Freud (1899) used this term to refer to early childhood memories employed as a screen onto which is projected subsequently occurring, repressed, and disguised wish-fulfilling sexual desire.

Secondary gain Term used by Freud to refer to 'motives of illness' (Freud, 1905a, p.42). While one motive involves gaining primary process, hallucinatory wish-fulfilment gain, the other motive secures actual or secondary process gain. Examples for Freud included the secondary gain his patient Dora (see Chapter 10) would have derived from her psychological ills if, for the sake of her health, she had succeeded in persuading her father to abandon his affair with his mistress, Frau K.

Secondary process Freud (e.g. 1911a) used this term to refer to reality-based conscious thinking in contrast to wish-fulfilling, primary process, unconscious thinking.

Secondary revision The dream-work process, according to Freud (e.g. 1900, 1901a), through which latent and unconscious wish-fulfilling dream thoughts are revised in their conscious and manifest recall in more or less coherent narrative form.

Structural theory In psychoanalysis this refers to Freud's (1923a) id-ego-superego theory or model of the mind.

Subconscious A term which Freud (1915b) explicitly rejected but which is often used to refer to what is unconscious.

Sublimation Term used by Freud (e.g. 1905b) to denote the diversion of the sexual drive into cultural pursuits such as artistic creation and intellectual enquiry.

Superego Agency of the mind first described by Freud (1923a) as formed through identification with the father or others as representative of socially given rules and demands, not least society's taboo on incest.

Taboo Anthropological term used by Freud (e.g.1913b) to signify socially agreed prohibited acts such as incest.

Thanatos Name of the Greek god of death which Freud (e.g.1920a, 1930) used to refer to the destructive death instinct in contrast to Eros signifying the constructive life instinct.

Topographical theory Freud's (e.g. 1915–1917) understanding of the mind as a tripartite – unconscious, preconscious, conscious – system.

Totem Anthropological term used by Freud (1913b) to refer to an animal representing the tribal ancestor of a clan.

Training analysis The psychoanalysis of a trainee psychoanalyst as part of their training.

Transference In psychoanalysis this refers to the process whereby the patient in psychoanalytic treatment experiences the psychoanalyst in terms of more or less unconscious experience of other significant figures in their life.

Trauma Refers in psychoanalysis to a psychologically upsetting event.

Unconscious Term used by Freud (e.g. 1915–1917) to characterize material which is repressed and, as such, unavailable to the preconscious or conscious mind.

Unconscious sense of guilt The result, according to Freud (e.g. 1925c), of conflict between the superego and ego and manifested as anxiety.

Voyeurism Active sexual pleasure in watching others. Freud (e.g. 1905b) contrasted it with the passive sexual pleasure of exhibitionism.

Wish fulfilment The aim, according to Freud (e.g.1900, 1911a), of latent, unconscious dream thoughts and of the primary process of mind.

Working through The process whereby, according to Freud (e.g.1914a), patients in psychoanalytic treatment process the implications of the psychoanalyst's understanding or interpretation of the unconscious cause of their psychological ills.

REFERENCES

ABBREVIATIONS

BJP = *British Journal of Psychotherapy*
IJP = *International Journal of Psychoanalysis*
SE1–24 = *Standard Edition of the Complete Psychological Works of Sigmund Freud.* London: Hogarth, 1966–1974

Ackerman, N. & Jahoda, M. (1950) The dynamic basis of anti-Semitic attitudes. *Psychoanalytic Quarterly*, 17:240–260
Adorno, T. et al. (1950) *The Authoritarian Personality.* New York: Harper
Aitken, K. & Trevarthen, C. (2002) Infant intersubjectivity. *Journal of Child Psychology and Psychiatry*, 42:3–48
Anon (2012) Sigmund Freud speaks. *Psychology*, 7 May, n.p. www.openculture.com/2012/05/sigmund_freud_speaks_the_only_known_recording_of_his_voice_1938.html
Appignanesi, L. & Forrester, J. (1992) *Freud's Women.* London: Weidenfeld & Nicholson
Bertolucci, B. (2001) How to kill your father. *The Observer*, 21 October
Bion, W. (1954) Notes on the theory of schizophrenia. *Second Thoughts.* London: Heinemann, 1967, pp.23–35
Bion, W. (1957) Differentiation of the psychotic from the non-psychotic personalities. *Second Thoughts.* London: Heinemann, pp.43–64
Bion, W. (1960) Alpha, 24 February. *Cogitations.* London: Karnac, 1991, pp.141–144

Bion, W. (1962a) A theory of thinking. *Second Thoughts*. London: Heinemann, 1967, pp. 110–119

Bion, W. (1962b) *Learning from Experience*. London: Heinemann

Bion, W. (1965) *Transformations*. London: Heinemann

Blenkiron, P. (1999) Who is suitable for cognitive behavioural therapy? *Journal of the Royal Society of Medicine*, 92(May):222–229

Boehlich, W. (1990) *The Letters of Sigmund Freud to Eduard Silberstein 1871–1881*. Cambridge, Massachusetts: Harvard University Press

Bott Spillius, E. (2001) Freud and Klein on the concept of phantasy. *IJP*, 82:361–373

Bowlby, J. (1953) *Child Care and the Growth of Love*. Harmondsworth: Penguin Books, 1965

Bowlby, J. (1969) *Attachment and Loss*. New York: Basic Books

Breuer, J. (1895a) Fräulein Anna O. SE2:19–47

Breuer, J. (1895b) Theoretical. SE2:183–251

Breuer, J. & Freud, S. (1893) On the psychical mechanism of hysterical phenomena. *Studies on Hysteria*. SE2:1–17

Chalk, N. (2013) Healthy babies suck thumb in womb. 8 October, www.express.co.uk/life-style/health/435110/Healthy-babies-suck-thumb-in-womb

Coren, A. (2009) *Short-Term Psychotherapy*. Basingstoke: Palgrave

Creed, B. (1993) *The Monstrous-Feminine: Film, Feminism, Psychoanalysis*. London & New York: Routledge

Cregeen, S. (2017) *Short-Term Psychoanalytic Psychotherapy for Adolescents with Moderate or Severe Depression*. London: Routledge

Cripwell, C. (2011) Finding the depressed object in the obsessional. *IJP*, 92:117–133

Davids, F. (2011) *Internal Racism*. Basingstoke: Palgrave Macmillan

Deutsch, F. (1957) A footnote to Freud's 'Fragment of an analysis of a case of hysteria'. In C. Bernheimer & C. Kahane (eds.) *In Dora's Case*. London: Virago, 1985, pp. 35–43

Doolittle, H. (1933) Diary entry, 9 March. *Tribute to Freud*. Manchester: Carcanet, 1885, pp. 145–147

Eagleton, T. (2017) Not just anybody. *London Review of Books*, 39, 5 January, pp. 35–37

Engels, F. (1884) *The Origin of the Family, Private Property, and the State*. London: Penguin Books

Fanon, F. (1952) *Black Skin, White Masks*. London: Pluto

Feaver, W. (2019) *The Lives of Lucian Freud*. London: Bloomsbury

Felski, R. (2015) *The Limits of Critique*. Chicago: University of Chicago Press

Flynn, S. et al. (2016) Homicide-suicide and the role of mental disorder. *Social Psychiatry & Psychiatric Epidemiology*, 51:877–884

Fonagy, P. (2001) *Attachment Theory and Psychoanalysis*. New York: Other Press

Fonagy, P. et al. (2015) Pragmatic randomized controlled trial of long-term psychoanalytic psychotherapy for treatment-resistant depression. *World Psychiatry*, 14:312–321

Forrester, J. (2016) *Thinking in Cases*. Cambridge: Polity

Foucault, M. (1976) *The History of Sexuality*. New York: Pantheon, 1978

Freud, A. (1926) Introduction to the technique of the analysis of children. *The Psycho-Analytical Treatment of Children*. London: Imago, 1946, pp. 3–52

Freud, A. (1936) *The Ego and the Mechanisms of Defence*. London: Hogarth, 1968

Freud, S. (1892–1899) Extracts from the Fliess papers. SE1:172–280

Freud, S. (1894) The neuro-psychoses of defence. SE3:45–61

Freud, S. (1895a) Project for a scientific psychology. SE1:281–397

Freud, S. (1895b) Case histories. SE2:48–181

Freud, S. (1895c) The psychotherapy of hysteria. SE2:253–305

Freud, S. (1896a) Letter to Fliess, 6 December. SE1:233–239

Freud, S. (1896b) The aetiology of hysteria. SE3:187–221

Freud, S. (1897) Letter to Fliess, 15 October. SE1:263–266

Freud, S. (1899) Screen memories. SE3:299–322

Freud, S. (1900) *The Interpretation of Dreams*. SE4–5

Freud, S. (1901a) *On Dreams*. SE5:629–686

Freud, S. (1901b) *The Psychopathology of Everyday Life*. SE6

Freud, S. (1905a) Fragment of an analysis of a case of hysteria. SE7:1–22

Freud, S. (1905b) *Three Essays on the Theory of Sexuality*. SE7:125–245

Freud, S. (1905c) On psychotherapy. SE7:255–268

Freud, S. (1905d) Jokes and their relation to the unconscious. SE8

Freud, S. (1907a) Delusions and dreams in Jensen's *Gradiva*. SE9:1–93

Freud, S. (1907b) Obsessive actions and religious practices. SE9:115–127

Freud, S. (1908a) Creative writers and day-dreaming. SE9:141–153

Freud, S. (1908b) Hysterical phantasies and their relation to bisexuality. SE9:155–166

Freud, S. (1908c) Character and anal erotism. SE9:167–175

Freud, S. (1908d) 'Civilized' sexual morality and modern nervous illness. SE9:177–204

Freud, S. (1908e) Letter to Jung, 13 August, in McGuire

Freud, S. (1909a) Analysis of a phobia in a five-year-old boy. SE10:1–147

Freud, S. (1909b) Notes upon a case of obsessional neurosis. SE10:151–318

Freud, S. (1910a) Five lectures on psycho-analysis. SE11:1–55

Freud, S. (1910b) Leonardo da Vinci and a memory of his childhood. SE11:57–137

Freud, S. (1910c) The future prospects of psycho-analytic therapy. SE11:139–151

Freud, S. (1910d) A special type of choice of object made by men. SE11:163–175

Freud, S. (1911a) Formulations on the two principles of mental functioning. SE12:213–226

Freud, S. (1911b) Psycho-analytic notes on an autobiographical account of a case of paranoia. SE12:1–79
Freud, S. (1912a) On the universal tendency to debasement in the sphere of love. SE11:177–190
Freud, S. (1912b) The dynamics of transference. SE12:99–108
Freud, S. (1912c) Recommendations to physicians practising psycho-analysis. SE12:109–120
Freud, S. (1913a) On beginning the treatment. SE12:121–144
Freud, S. (1913b) *Totem and Taboo*. SE13:1–161
Freud, S. (1914a) Remembering, repeating and working-through. SE12:145–156
Freud, S. (1914b) On the history of the psycho-analytic movement. SE14:1–66
Freud, S. (1914c) On narcissism. SE14:67–102
Freud, S. (1914d) The Moses of Michelangelo. SE13:211–238
Freud, S. (1915a) Instincts and their vicissitudes. SE14:109–140
Freud, S. (1915b) Repression. SE14:141–158
Freud, S. (1915c) The unconscious. SE14:159–215
Freud, S. (1915d) Mourning and melancholia. *SE14*:237–258
Freud, S. (1915e) Thoughts for the times on war and death. SE14:273–300
Freud, S. (1915–1917) *Introductory Lectures on Psycho-Analysis*. SE15 & SE16
Freud, S. (1916) Some character-types met within psychoanalytic work. SE14:309–333
Freud, S. (1917) Mourning and melancholia. SE14:237–258
Freud, S. (1918a) The taboo of virginity. SE11:191–208
Freud, S. (1918b) From the history of an infantile neurosis. SE17:1–122
Freud, S. (1918c) Letter to Pfister, 9 October. In Meng & Freud
Freud, S. (1919) The 'uncanny'. SE17: 217–256
Freud, S. (1920a) Beyond the pleasure principle. SE18:1–64
Freud, S. (1920b) The psychogenesis of a case of female homosexuality. SE18:145–172
Freud, S. (1921) Group psychology and the analysis of the ego. SE18:65–143
Freud, S. (1923a) The ego and the id. SE19:1–66
Freud, S. (1923b) The infantile genital organization. SE19:139–145
Freud, S. (1924) Neurosis and psychosis. SE19:147–153
Freud, S. (1925a) Negation. SE19:233–239
Freud, S. (1925b) Some psychical consequences of the anatomical distinction between the sexes. SE19:248–258
Freud, S. (1925c) An autobiographical study. SE20:1–70
Freud, S. (1926) Address to the Society of B'nai B'rith. SE20:271–274
Freud, S. (1927a) The future of an illusion. SE21:1–56
Freud, S. (1927b) Fetishism. SE21:147–157
Freud, S. (1928) Dostoevsky and parricide. SE21:173–194

Freud, S. (1930) Civilization and its discontents. SE21:57–145
Freud, S. (1931) Female sexuality. SE21:221–243
Freud, S. (1933a) *New Introductory Lectures on Psycho-Analysis*. SE22:1–182
Freud, S. (1933b) Letter to Albert Einstein, September. SE22:203–215
Freud, S. (1935) Letter to an American mother. *American Journal of Psychiatry*, 1951, 107:787
Freud, S. (1937a) Analysis terminable and interminable. SE23:209–253
Freud, S. (1937b) Constructions in analysis. SE23:255–269
Freud, S. (1938) Anti-Semitism in England. SE23:301
Freud, S. (1939) Moses and monotheism. SE23:1–137
Frosh, S. (2016) Studies in prejudice: theorizing anti-Semitism in the wake of the Nazi holocaust. In M. Ffytche & D. Pick (eds.) *Psychoanalysis in the Age of Totalitarianism*. London & New York: Routledge
Gammeltoft, T. & Segal, L.B. (2016) Anthropology and psychoanalysis. *Ethos*, 44:399–410
Gardiner, M. (1972) *The Wolf Man*. New York: Basic Books
Gay, P. (1988) *Freud: A Life for Our Time*. London: Dent
Gombrich, E. (1954) Psychoanalysis and the history of art. *IJP*, 35:401–411
Groddeck, G. (1923) *Das Buch vom Es (The Book of the It)*. Vienna: Internationaler Psychoanalytischer Verlag
Hartmann, H. (1939) Ego psychology and the problem of adaptation. *Psychoanalytic Quarterly*, 1989, 58:526–550
Hartmann, H. (1964) *Essays on Ego Psychology*. New York: International Universities Press
Heimann, P. (1950) On counter-transference. *IJP*, 31:81–84
Holmes, J. (2015) Attachment theory in clinical practice. *IJP*, 31:208–228
Horney, K. (1926) The flight from womanhood. *Feminine Psychology*. New York: Norton, 1967:54–70
Isaacs, S. (1948) The nature and function of phantasy. *IJP*, 29:73–97
Jones, E. (1953) *Sigmund Freud: The Young Freud*. London: Hogarth
Jones, E. (1961) *The Life and Work of Sigmund Freud*. New York: Basic Books
Jung, C.G. (1912a) *Symbols of Transformation*. New York: Bollingen, 1956
Jung, C.G. (1912b) Letter to Freud, 11 November, in McGuire.
Jung, C.G. (1913a) Psychoanalysis and neurosis. *Collected Works of C.G. Jung, Volume 4*. London: Routledge, 1961:243–251
Jung, C.G. (1913b) A contribution to the study of psychological types. *Psychological Types*. London & New York: Routledge, 2017:455–464
Jung, C.G. (1933) *Modern Man in Search of a Soul*. London: Routledge, 1984
Klein, M. (1921) The development of a child. *Love, Guilt and Reparation*. London: Hogarth, 1975:1–53

Klein, M. (1928) Early stages of the Oedipus conflict. *Love, Guilt and Reparation.* London: Hogarth, pp.186–198

Klein, M. (1935) A contribution to the psychogenesis of manic-depressive states. *Love, Guilt and Reparation.* London: Hogarth, 1975:262–289

Klein, M. (1940) Mourning and its relation to manic-depressive states. *Love, Guilt and Reparation.* London: Hogarth, pp.344–369

Klein, M. (1945) The Oedipus complex in the light of early anxieties. *Love, Guilt and Reparation.* London: Hogarth, pp.370–419

Klein, M. (1946) Some schizoid mechanisms. *Envy and Gratitude.* London: Hogarth, 1975:1–24

Knekt, P. et al. (2008) Randomized trial on the effectiveness of long- and short-term psychodynamic psychotherapy and solution-focused therapy on psychiatric symptoms during a 3-year follow-up. *Psychological Medicine*, 38:689–703

Koedt, A. (1970) *The Myth of the Vaginal Orgasm.* Somerville, Massachusetts: New England Free Press

Kohut, H. (1971) *The Analysis of the Self.* New York: International Universities Press

Kris, E. (1952) *Psychoanalytic Explorations in Art.* New York: International Universities Press

Kristeva, J. (1980) Giotto's Joy. *Desire in Language.* New York: Columbia University Press, pp.210–236

Kristeva, J. (1982) *Powers of Horror: An Essay on Abjection.* New York: Columbia University Press

Kristeva, J. (1984) *Revolution in Poetic Language.* New York: Columbia University Press

Lacan, J. (1948) Aggressivity in psychoanalysis. *Ecrits.* London: Tavistock, 1977:8–29

Lacan, J. (1949) The mirror stage as formative of the function of the I as revealed in psychoanalytic experience. *Ecrits.* London: Tavistock, pp.1–7

Lacan, J. (1955-1956) On a question preliminary to any possible treatment of psychosis. *Ecrits.* London: Tavistock, pp.179–225

Lacan, J. (1958) The signification of the phallus. *Ecrits.* London: Tavistock, pp.281–291

Laing, R.D. & Esterson, A. (1964) *Sanity, Madness and the Family.* London: Tavistock

Laplanche, J. (1999) *Essays on Otherness.* London: Routledge

Laplanche, J. & Pontalis, J-B. (1968) Fantasy and the origins of sexuality. *IJP*, 49:1–18

Laplanche, J. & Pontalis, J-B. (1980) *The Language of Psycho-Analysis.* London: Hogarth

Lasch, C. (1979) *The Culture of Narcissism.* New York: Norton

Lear, J. (2000) *Happiness, Death, and the Remainder of Life.* Cambridge, Massachusetts: Harvard University Press

Lear, J. (2005) *Freud*. London & New York: Routledge
Lemma, A. (2013) The body one has and the body one is. *IJP*, 94:277–292
Lemma, A. (2018) Transitory identities. *IJP*, 99:1089–1106
Leuzinger-Bohleber, M. et al. (2019) How to measure psychic transformations in long-term treatments of chronically depressed patients. *IJP*, 100:99–127
Lévi-Straus, C. (1949) *The Elementary Structures of Kinship*. Boston: Beacon Press, 1969
Levine, H. (2012) The colourless canvas. *IJP*, 93:607–629
Light, A. (2019) *A Radical Romance*. London: Penguin Books
Lombardi, R. (2005) On the psychoanalytic treatment of a psychotic breakdown. *Psychoanalytic Quarterly*, 74:1069–1099
Lombardi, R. & Pola, M. (2010) The body, adolescence, and psychosis. *IJP*, 91:1419–1444
Longhofer, J. (2015) *A-Z of Psychodynamic Practice*. London & New York: Palgrave
McGuire, W. (ed.) *The Freud-Jung Letters*. London: Hogarth, 1974
Malan, D. (1963) *A Study of Brief Psychotherapy*. London: Tavistock
Malinowski, B. (1927) *Sex and Repression in Savage Society*. London: Routledge & Kegan Paul
Martindale, B. (2015) The dynamics of psychosis: Therapeutic implications. *Psychiatric Times*, 20 January. www.psychiatrictimes.com/
Martindale, B. & Summers, A. (2013) The psychodynamics of psychosis. *Advances in Psychiatric Treatment*, 19:124–131
McGuire, W. (1974) *The Freud-Jung Letters*. London: Hogarth
Meng, H. & Freud, E. (1963) *Psycho-Analysis and Faith*. London: Hogarth
Milner, M. (1950) *On Not Being Able to Paint*. London: Heinemann
Milner, M. (1952) Aspects of symbolism in comprehension of the not-self. *IJP* 33:181–195
Milner, M. (1955) The communication of primary sensual experience. *The Suppressed Madness of Sane Men*. London: Routledge, 1987:114–167
Milton, J. et al. (2011) *A Short Introduction to Psychoanalysis*. London: SAGE
Mitchell, J. (1974) *Psychoanalysis and Feminism*. London: Allen Lane
Mosher, D. (2008) Incest not so taboo in nature. livescience.com/2226-incest-taboo-nature-html
Mulvey, L. (1975) Visual pleasure and narrative cinema. *Screen*, 16:6–18
Newbigin, J. (2015) Rethinking our approach to sexualities. *New Associations*, Spring:1–2
O'Connor, N. & Ryan, J. (1993) *Wild Desires and Mistaken Identities*. London: Virago
Office for National Statistics (2016) *Crime Survey for England and Wales*. Quoted in IICSA (Independent Inquiry into Child Sexual Abuse) www.iicsa.org.uk/publications/inquiry/interim/nature-effects-child-sexual-abuse/scale-child-sexual-abuse-england-wales#IicsaReferencesReference2

Ogden, T. (1994) The analytic third: Working with intersubjective clinical facts. *IJP*, 75:3–19

Pater, W. (1873) *Studies in the History of the Renaissance*. London: Macmillan

Pfister, O. (1918) Letter from Oskar Pfister to Sigmund Freud, October 29. *IJP*, 59:63

Poyet, P. (2019) Working through centred on the body in the analysis of a psychotic adolescent. *IJP*, 100:463–480

Quinodoz, J.-M. (2005) *Reading Freud*. London & New York: Routledge

Radcliffe, J. & Yeomans, F. (2019) Transference-focused psychotherapy for patients with personality disorders. *BJP*, 35:4–23

Reich, W. (1933) *The Mass Psychology of Fascism*. New York: Farrar, Straus & Giroux, 1980

Rivers, W.H.R. (1918) The repression of war experience. *Proceedings of the Royal Society of Medicine*, 11:1–20

Riviere, J. (1936) A contribution to the analysis of the negative therapeutic reaction. *IJP*, 17: 304–320

Roudinesco, E. (2016) *Freud: In His Time and Ours*. Cambridge, Massachusetts: Harvard University Press

Ryan, J. (2017) *Class and Psychoanalysis*. London & New York: Routledge

Rycroft, C. (1968) *A Critical Dictionary of Psychoanalysis*. Harmondsworth: Penguin

Sabbadini, A. (2016) Cinema (film) and psychoanalysis. *The Routledge Handbook of Psychoanalysis in the Social Sciences and Humanities*. London & New York: Routledge, pp. 333–347

Salomonssen, B. (2012) Has infantile sexuality anything to do with infants? *IJP*, 93:631–647

Sayers, J. (1997) *Freudian Tales*. London: Vintage

Schatzman, M. (1973) *Soul-Murder: Persecution in the Family*. New York: Random House

Schaverien, J. (2015) *Boarding School Syndrome*. London: Routledge

Schechter, K. (2010) The soldiers project. *IJP*, 91:1239–1241

Schneider, J. (2010) From Freud's dream-work to Bion's work of dreaming. *IJP*, 91:521–540

Segal, H. (1952) A psychoanalytic approach to aesthetics. *The Work of Hanna Segal*. New York & London: Jason Aronson, 1981, pp. 185–206

Segal, H. (1957) Notes on symbol formation. *The Work of Hanna Segal*. New York & London: Jason Aronson, pp. 49–65

Segal, H. (1984) Joseph Conrad and the mid-life crisis. *Psychoanalysis, Literature and War*. London: Routledge, 1997, pp. 123–132

Shedler, J. (2010) The efficacy of psychodynamic psychotherapy. *American Psychologist*, 65:98–109

Smith, D. (2003) *Psychoanalysis in Focus*. London: SAGE

Solms, M. & Turnbull, O. (2002) *The Brain and the Inner World*. London: Karnac

Sontag, S. (1966) *Against Interpretation*. New York: Farrar, Straus and Giroux

Stokes, A. (1934) *Stones of Rimini*. In L. Gowing (ed.) *The Critical Writings of Adrian Stokes, Volume I*. London: Thames & Hudson, 1978, pp.181–301

Stokes, A. (1955) Form in art. In M. Klein, P. Heimann, & R.E. Money-Kyrle (eds.) *New Directions in Psycho-Analysis*. London: Tavistock, pp.406–420

Target, M. (2007) Is our sexuality our own? *BJP*, 23:517–530

Townsend, P. (2019) *Creative States of Mind: Psychoanalysis and the Artist's Process*. London & New York: Routledge

Trevarthen, C. & Aitken, K.J. (2001) Infant intersubjectivity: Research, theory, and clinical applications. *Journal of Child Psychology and Psychiatry*, 42:3–48

Tyler, I. (2013) *Revolting Subjects: Social Abjection and Resistance in Neoliberal Britain*. London: Zed Books

Ward, I. (1997) Race and racism. *British Journal of Psychotherapy*, 14:91–97

Winnicott, D.W. (1945) Primitive emotional development. *Collected Papers*. London: Tavistock, 1958, pp.229–142

Winnicott, D.W. (1951) Transitional objects and transitional phenomena. *Collected Papers*. London: Tavistock, 1958, pp.229–242

Winnicott, D.W. (1953) Symptom tolerance in paediatrics. *Collected Papers*. London: Tavistock, pp.101–117

Zweig, S. (1927) *Twenty-Four Hours in the Life of a Woman*. London: Pushkin Press, 2003

INDEX

Note: See Glossary for further details about the meaning of some of the items in this index.

abreaction 9
Ackerman, Nathan 187
active (as opposite of passive) 48, 90, 136, 139, 183
adolescence 52, 121
Adorno, Theodor 178, 188
affect 14, 21, 121, 122
aggression 45, 122, 146, 148–149, 176–179
aim, sexual 47–48, 51, 99, 153, 183
Aitken, Kenneth 109
ambivalence 117, 163
anality 27, 48, 50–51, 53–54, 73–75, 86, 91, 112–113
analytic couch 71, 73, 115, 120
anatomy 1, 6–7, 26, 122, 166, 170
anger 35, 65, 75, 123, 134–135, 138, 148–149, 188–189
Anna O 8–12, 17, 102, 133
anthropology 151, 162–168, 191

anti-Semitism 3–4, 145, 151, 178, 186–189
anxiety 10, 18, 20, 52, 55, 64–66, 69, 88–89, 101, 121, 134, 140, 144, 150, 161, 187–189
aphasia 1, 7
Appignanesi, Lisa 10, 62
art 5, 37, 77, 98, 151, 153–162, 168, 175–176, 191
assessment 120–121, 123
attachment 27, 62, 81, 93, 101, 103, 108–110, 119, 124, 130, 132, 182
autoeroticism 80

Barker, Pat 137
bereavement 128–129; *see also* grief
Berlin 6
Bernays, Martha 1, 6–7, 180; *see also* Freud, Martha
Bernheim, Hippolyte 12

Bernheimer, Charles 62
Bertolucci, Bernardo 156
biography 46, 89, 98, 151, 153, 155–156, 161, 169
Bion, Wilfred 78, 82, 119, 159
bipolar disorder 131
bisexuality 139, 180, 183, 185
blank screen (tabula rasa) 116
Bleuler, Eugen 95
Boltraffio 37
Bonaparte, Princess Marie 187
Bosnia–Herzegovina 37–38
Botticelli 37–38
Bowlby, John 108, 119, 132
breast 35, 49, 52, 81, 103, 154, 173
Brentano, Franz 170
Breuer, Josef 1, 6, 8–12, 17, 102, 133, 180–181, 190
Brücke, Ernst 6
Brunswick, Ruth Mack 89
Burghölzli 95–96

castration 51, 56, 86, 88–89, 91, 138–143, 150, 167–168, 181
catharsis 9
Charcot, Martin 1, 6–7
childbirth 51, 166, 168
Christianity 4, 166, 171
Christmas 44, 50, 86, 87
civilization 97, 172, 174–180
clan societies 162, 164–167
Claus, Carl 5
clitoris 51, 140
cocaine 1, 6, 26
cognitive behavioural therapy (CBT) 122–124
communism 177
compulsion 23, 70, 88, 90, 135, 137, 163, 170; *see also* obsession
condensation 34, 43–45
conflict 14, 42, 121

Conrad, Joseph 156
conscience 143, 177–178
consciousness 9, 12, 15, 24–25, 27, 36–37, 39, 42–43, 45–46, 54, 56–57, 61, 68–69, 72–75, 78, 90, 96, 100–101, 109, 112, 114, 143–144, 159–160, 163, 171, 178, 188, 190
containment 75, 82, 119, 160
Coren, Alex 120–121
countertransference 117–119
Creed, Barbara 168
criminality 22, 71–72, 184
Cripwell, Claire 75
Cronenberg, David 157
Csonka, Margarethe 113, 181

Dali, Salvador 157
Darwin, Charles 165
Davids, Fakhry 188–189
day-dreaming 9, 11–12, 181
death instinct 125, 133, 135, 137, 139, 150, 176
debt 72, 83, 163, 167
defecation 175
defence 21, 80–82, 84, 112, 122–123, 125, 130, 132, 139–140, 143–145, 150, 173, 179, 181, 183, 187–189
deferred action 17
delusion 76–83, 91, 112, 129, 131, 144, 171, 176
dementia 111
dementia praecox 76, 96
demons 29, 164
dependence 132, 145, 189
depression 57, 121, 123, 125, 127, 129, 131–132, 139, 143, 148, 150; *see also* melancholia
desire, sexual 16, 22–24, 34, 52, 59–60, 79–80, 88–89, 98, 105, 107,

112, 139–140, 154, 157, 181, 183; *see also* wish
Deutsch, Felix 62
Deutsch, Helene 182
diagnosis 22, 70, 83, 111–112, 116, 131, 133, 171
Dickens, Charles 128
disguise 24, 27, 34–36, 45–46, 112
disgust 8, 18, 51, 57–58, 70, 175
displacement 34, 44–45, 55, 58, 90, 163, 188
Doolittle, Hilda 182
Dora 55, 57–63, 76, 90, 112, 115
Dostoevsky, Fyodor 151, 156
dream 9–11, 27, 29–37, 42–43, 45–47, 54–55, 59–60, 62, 64–65, 67, 77–79, 87–88, 90, 95–96, 98, 100, 102–105, 116, 120, 123, 131, 138, 154–155, 157–159, 167, 171, 179, 187; *see also* day-dreaming
dream-work 34–36, 43–46, 159
drive *see* instinct
dynamics 24–27, 36–37, 39, 42–43, 54, 101, 167, 179, 188, 191

Eckstein, Emma 17, 31
education 171–172
ego 99, 101, 125, 130–131, 139–146, 149–150, 173, 177–178
ego ideal 130, 139
ego psychology 125, 145–146, 149–150
Elisabeth von R 13–15, 17, 114
emotion 15, 21, 101, 117, 133, 141, 148
empathy 149
Engels, Friedrich 167
Eros 176–177
eroticism 1, 14, 16, 26, 51, 68, 73–74, 79–80, 106, 155, 178

errors (*or* Freudian slips) 37, 39–40, 43, 47, 54
Esterson, Aaron 81
evenly suspended attention 114–115, 120
exhibitionism 48, 99
extrovert 97

false memory syndrome 22
Fanon, Frantz 188
fantasy 1, 20, 23, 25–26, 65, 67, 153–155, 158; *see also* phantasy
Fascism 145, 178
father 143, 146, 156–157, 163–165, 167, 169–173, 177–178, 181–182, 186, 189; *see also* patriarchy
father-complex 72, 81, 84, 96
fear 55, 64, 70, 72–73, 89–90, 121, 132, 144, 149, 163–164, 166, 172–173, 189; *see also* anxiety
Feaver, William 156
Felski, Ruth 161
femininity 139–140, 168, 175, 181, 183
feminism 185
Ferenczi, Sandor 79, 96
fetishism 111
film 160
fixation 112
Flechsig, Paul 76–82, 112
Fleischl-Marxow, Ernst von 6
Fliess, Wilhelm 18, 22–23, 34–35
Fluss, Gisela 24, 39
Fonagy, Peter 109, 119, 132
forgetting 37–39, 108, 134
Forrester, John 10, 62, 90
fort-da game 125, 136–138
Frazer, J.G. 162
free association 13–14, 18–19, 30–31, 35–36, 39, 54, 59–60, 73, 87, 100, 104, 114–116, 120, 123, 158

Freiburg 3–4, 7, 24
Freud, Amalia (Freud's mother) 3
Freud, Anna (Freud's daughter) 7, 31–32, 69, 145, 170, 187
Freud, Emanuel (Freud's half-brother) 5
Freud, Ernst (Freud's grandson) 135–138
Freud, Jacob (Freud's father) 3, 5, 169–170
Freud, Lucian (Freud's grandson) 156
Freud, Martha (Freud's wife) 170, 187; *see also* Bernays, Martha
Freud, Philipp (Freud's half-brother) 3, 5, 24, 40
Frosh, Stephen 188
Freudian slips (*or* errors) 37, 39–40, 43, 47, 54

Gammeltoft, Tine 167
Gardiner, Muriel 89
Gay, Peter 4, 22, 46, 89
gender 151, 179–180, 183, 191
genitality 18–19, 27, 47–48, 51, 53–54, 58–59, 80, 86–87, 103–104, 109, 113, 167, 175–176, 181
Giotto 160
God 78–79, 81, 131, 157, 166, 169–171
gods 29, 172, 195, 204
Gombrich, Ernst 155
governess 13, 61, 85–86, 112
Graf, Max 63, 68–69
grandiosity 131
grief 15, 128–129; *see also* bereavement
Groddeck, Georg 142
guilt 17, 21, 72, 129–130, 143–144, 156–157, 163, 165, 170, 177–178, 181

hallucination 10, 33–35, 76, 83, 133
Hammerschlag, Samuel 170
Hans 55, 63–69, 76, 90, 101, 106–107, 112–113, 120, 138, 163–164
Hartmann, Heinz 145
hatred 55, 72–75, 80–82, 90, 112, 107, 125, 127, 129–132, 143, 148, 150, 156, 163–164, 171, 188
Heimann, Paula 118
heterosexuality 48, 113, 121, 139, 183–184
Hitchcock, Alfred 157
Hitler, Adolf 178, 187
Holmes, Jeremy 109, 132
Holy Communion 166
homosexuality 79–80, 112–113, 139, 154, 176, 183–185
Hönig, Olga 63
Horney, Karin 181
horror 71, 158, 162–163, 167–168
hostility 45–46, 141, 164, 166, 177, 181, 189
Hug-Hellmuth, Hermine 68
hunger 32, 35, 48, 99
hypnoid state 9, 11–12, 181
hypnosis 6, 8–10, 12–13, 16, 26
hypomania *see* mania
hysteria 1, 6–13, 15–23, 25–26, 47, 57–58, 62, 95, 101–102, 133, 144, 174, 181

Ibsen, Henrik 151, 157
id–ego–superego model 125, 142, 146, 149–150
identification 40, 58, 81, 121, 125, 130, 132, 139–140, 143, 145–146, 150, 156, 160, 177, 178, 181, 188–189
image 37, 49, 86, 88, 105, 136, 145
imaginary 146

imagination 59, 60, 65, 67–68, 71, 86, 137, 174–175, 181
incest 27, 52–53, 139–140, 143, 162, 164–165, 167, 176
infant sexuality 18–19, 23, 47–54, 106–110, 116, 139, 174, 183
infantile amnesia 51
inhibition 36, 171–172
inner world 81, 97, 119, 146, 148, 178
instinct (or drive) 45, 47–48, 68, 80, 99–101, 125, 135, 137, 139, 150, 153, 155, 175–178, 190
intercourse, sexual 68, 70, 72, 77, 87–88, 105, 107, 113, 139, 166, 175
internalization 119
interpretation 27, 29–31, 36, 54, 59, 65–66, 73–75, 96, 102, 104–105, 113, 116–120, 123, 136, 138, 144, 148–149, 151, 154, 159–161, 167, 179, 189
introjection 130, 139, 188–189
introvert 97

Jahoda, Marie 187
jealousy 1, 22–23, 41, 59, 140, 157, 165
Jewishness 3–5, 44, 46, 169–172, 187–188
joke-work 44–45
jokes 27, 43–47, 54, 100
Jones, Ernest 169, 180
Jung, Carl Gustav 30, 79, 93, 95–99, 102, 108, 115, 117, 124, 157, 162

Kahane, Claire 62
Klein, Melanie 69, 81–82, 131–132, 146–147, 150, 181
Knekt, Paul 122
Koedt, Anne 51

Kohut, Heinz 145
Koller, Carl 6
Krafft-Ebing, Richard 20, 48
Kris, Ernst 145
Kristeva, Julia 160, 167–168, 173

Lacan, Jacques 104–105, 145–146, 167–168
Lahire, Bernard 179
Laing, Ronnie 81–82
Lampl-de Groot, Jeanne 182
Lang, Andrew 162
Lanzer, Ernst 55, 70–76, 90, 96, 112, 115, 134, 163, 171
Laplanche, Jean 109–110
Lasch, Christopher 178
latency 27, 51, 197, 202
latent content 34, 36
Leader, Darian 81
Lear, Jonathan 62, 136–137
Leipzig 3, 22, 76–78
Lemma, Alessandra 185
Leonardo da Vinci 151, 153–156, 184
lesbianism 180, 183–185
Leuzinger-Bohleber, Marianne 123
Lévi-Strauss, Claude 167
Levine, Howard 160
libido 22, 97, 112, 171
Light, Alison 128
literature 153, 156–161, 191
Lombardi, Riccardo 82
London 41, 97, 120, 151, 187–188, 202
loss 37, 52, 79, 89, 121–122, 128–130, 132, 137, 139, 143, 178
love 1, 6, 13, 15, 23–24, 39, 52–53, 55, 60–61, 72, 74–75, 80–81, 87, 90, 98–99, 112, 117, 125, 130–132, 135, 139, 140, 143, 150, 156–157, 163, 171, 173–174, 176, 180

Lowenstein, Rudolph 145
Lucy R 13, 17, 114

madness 81, 176
magic 164
Mahler, Gustav 5
Malan, David 120
Malinowski, Bronislaw 167
mania 122, 131–132
manifest dream 34, 36
Martindale, Brian 82–83
Marx, Karl 167
masculinity 121, 139–140, 166, 181–183
masochism 48, 99, 119
Massachusetts 68, 96
masturbation 21, 70, 72, 104, 107, 140, 157, 175
matriarchy 167
medicine 1, 6, 26, 30, 32, 42, 79, 82–83, 95, 114, 122, 170
melancholia 127, 129–132, 139, 143–144, 150; *see also* depression
memory 1, 13–14, 19–26, 33, 39, 72, 77, 87–88, 101, 120, 134, 154, 159, 175, 182
menstruation 166, 168
metapsychology 99
Meynert, Theodor 6
Michelangelo 151, 157–158, 184
Milner, Marion 50, 159, 173
Milton, Jane 118–119
mirror stage 145–146
Mitchell, Juliet 183
Monet, Claude 159
morality 8, 51, 175–176
Morgan, David 179
Moses 151, 157–158, 173, 182, 187
mother 1, 5, 10, 14, 22–23, 27, 40, 42, 49–50, 52, 59–60, 63–69, 72–73, 75, 81, 83, 87–89, 97, 101, 106–109, 113, 117, 121–122, 125, 132, 136–140, 146, 154, 156–157, 163–165, 168, 171, 173, 181–182, 184, 189
mourning 127–129, 132, 163–164; *see also* bereavement and grief
movie 160
Mulvey, Laura 160

narcissism 79–81, 98, 112–113, 130–131, 144, 154, 157, 173, 181, 183, 186, 189
neurology (or neuroscience) 6, 29, 33, 35, 95, 190
neurosis 18, 20–21, 47–48, 52–53, 88, 96–97, 100, 108, 112–113, 144, 166, 171–172, 175, 181, 186
Newbigin, Juliet 184
nightmare 35, 55, 87–89, 133, 135, 137, 139, 176

object relations 119, 125, 143, 146, 148–149
object, sexual 48, 52, 80, 99, 106, 112, 154, 176
obsessional neurosis 20, 55, 70–75, 88–90, 163, 170–173
oceanic feeling 172–173
O'Connor, Noreen 183
Oedipus 1, 22–23, 25, 55, 67, 88
Ogden, Thomas 119
omnipotence 132, 164
orality 19, 27, 47–51, 53–54, 58, 112–113

Pankejeff, Sergei 55, 85–89, 91, 113, 115, 171–172
Pappenheim, Berthe 10
paranoia 20, 79–83, 91, 112
Paris 1, 6–7, 187

passive (as opposite of active) 48, 88, 99, 118, 136, 139, 183
Pater, Walter 154
patriarchy 105, 165, 167–168, 179, 182–183
penis 51, 63, 65–67, 86, 88–89, 103–106, 139–140, 154, 167
penis envy 51, 139–142, 150, 166, 181, 183, 185
perversion 20–21, 47–48, 51, 53, 111–113, 176, 183
Pfister, Oskar 171–172
phantasy 4, 21, 23, 61, 79, 104, 107, 155, 158, 172; *see also* fantasy
phobia 17, 55, 64–69, 90, 112, 163
physiology 1, 6–7, 26, 170
pleasure 45, 48–51, 71, 74, 96, 99, 154, 158
Pola, Marisa 82
politics 4, 42, 77, 151, 179–180, 191
Poyet, Pierrette 82
preconscious 100–101, 143
pregnancy 39, 42, 166
pressure technique 12–13, 16, 26, 114
primal scene 87–88
primary process 36–37, 96
projection 23, 80–82, 84, 112, 116, 119, 122, 130, 148, 164, 183, 188–189
Proust, Marcel 156
psychiatry 6, 48, 76–77, 81–83, 89, 95, 109, 111, 114, 120, 122, 132–133, 188
psychosexual development 48, 50–51, 70, 79–80, 86, 93, 107, 111–113, 124, 130, 167, 184, 191
psychosis 21, 76, 78, 81–84, 95–96, 104, 131, 144
psychotherapy 119–120, 148, 156, 183; *see also* treatment
puberty 18, 27, 47, 51, 53, 107, 112, 166, 174

Quinodoz, Jean-Michel 62, 75

racism 151, 186–189
Radcliffe, Jonathan 148
Rank, Otto 162
regression 53, 81, 86, 98, 111–113, 130–131, 183
Reich, Wilhelm 178
religion 88, 143, 151, 169–173, 176, 191
repetition compulsion 125, 135, 137, 150
repression 1, 12–16, 19–22, 24–27, 29, 34, 36, 39–41, 46, 54, 56, 73–75, 80, 84, 90, 93, 95, 99–101, 112–114, 116, 124, 130, 133, 143–144, 146, 154, 157–158, 161, 163–165, 167, 170–171, 174–176, 178–179, 181–183
resistance 12–13, 15–16, 26, 74, 101, 143, 157, 190
reversal 80, 84, 99, 112, 130, 183
ritual 88, 164–166, 170–173
Rivers, W H R 133–134, 137
Rolland, Romain 172
Roudinesco, Elisabeth 4, 46
Ryan, Joanna 179, 183

Sabbadini, Andrea 160
Sachs, Hanns 162
sadism 48, 86, 99
Salomonsson, Björn 109
Schatzman, Morton 82
Schaverien, Joy 133
schizophrenia 55, 76, 78, 80–85, 91, 95–96, 98, 103–104, 119
Schneider, John 160
Schnitzler, Arthur 5
Schreber, Daniel Paul 55, 76–85, 91, 96, 98, 112, 171, 183
screen memory 24, 39

secondary process 36–37, 96
secondary revision 35
seduction 1, 18–21, 25–26, 86, 93, 109
Segal, Hanna 104, 156
Segal, Lotte 167
self-analysis 22–23, 40, 63, 90, 118
sexual abuse 1, 17–23, 25–26, 78, 109, 112, 174
Shakespeare, William 151, 157
Shedler, Jonathan 123
Silberstein, Eduard 170
social class 174–175, 178–181, 186
sociology 151, 168, 174–175, 178–179, 181, 191
Solms, Mark 33
Sontag, Susan 160
Sophocles 151, 156, 158
Spielrein, Sabina 117, 157
Stokes, Adrian 158, 173
structural model 150
sublimation 51, 74, 153, 155, 175
suicide 38, 57, 60, 76, 113, 130–131
Summers, Alison 82
superego 9, 119, 125, 139–150, 156, 177–179, 181, 186
Svevo, Italo 157
symbol 8, 30, 93, 96–97, 102–106, 124, 136, 138, 145–146, 154, 166–167

taboo 27, 52–53, 162–168, 176
tabula rasa (blank screen) 116
talking cure 8, 10, 12, 104, 134, 137, 143
Target, Mary 109
Thanatos 176–177
thirst 48, 99
thumbsucking 48–49, 58, 112
topographical model 100–101
totem 162, 164–168

Townsend, Patricia 156
transference 55, 61–62, 73, 77, 79, 81, 90, 100, 115–120, 123, 145, 181–182
trauma 8–12, 18, 87, 102, 111, 122, 125, 133–137, 139–140, 150, 174
treatment 6–10, 12–13, 15, 26, 35, 55, 57–63, 68, 70–71, 73, 74–75, 78, 81–82, 88–90, 93, 101, 104, 114–124, 132–134, 137, 143–146, 148–149, 159, 178, 184, 188, 190; *see also* psychotherapy
Trevarthen, Colwyn 109
Turnbull, Oliver 33
Tyler, Imogen 168

uncanny 164
unconscious 1, 9, 11–13, 15–16, 19, 21, 24–27, 29–30, 32–46, 54–55, 61, 68, 72–75, 90, 96, 100–101, 109, 112, 114–116, 123, 125, 133, 142–144, 146, 154, 159–160, 163–164, 167, 171, 174–175, 178–179, 188, 190
Ungar, Virginia 183

vagina 51, 103
Vienna 1, 3–7, 10, 14, 22, 32, 66, 95, 151, 187, 190
voyeurism 48, 99

Welles, Orson 157
Wheelis, Allen 104
Winnicott, Donald 50, 108, 159
wish 1, 14, 20, 23–26, 31–36, 40, 42–43, 45–46, 51, 54, 60, 65–66, 68–69, 74, 107–108, 113, 121, 123, 125, 138–140, 143, 154–155, 159, 163–165, 167, 188; *see also* desire

Zurich 95
Zweig, Stefan 5, 157

Printed in Great Britain
by Amazon